U0510140

河南省文物考古研究院学术文库 乙种第32号
Henan Provincial Institute of Cultural Heritage and Archaeology
Academic Library Type B No.32

豫见东非 中肯考古
博戈里亚湖遗址石制品研究

FROM HENAN TO EAST AFRICA
SINO-KENYA PALEOLITHIC ARCHAEOLOGICAL PROJECT
A Study on Stone Artifacts from Lake Bogoria Site

编 著

河南省文物考古研究院
洛阳市考古研究院
肯尼亚国家博物馆

by
Henan Provincial Institute of Cultural Heritage and Archaeology
Luoyang City Cultural Relics and Archaeology Research Institute
National Museums of Kenya

文物出版社

图书在版编目（CIP）数据

豫见东非 中肯考古：博戈里亚湖遗址石制品研究：汉英对照 / 河南省文物考古研究院，洛阳市考古研究院，肯尼亚国家博物馆编著. -- 北京：文物出版社，2024.10. -- ISBN 978-7-5010-8525-5

Ⅰ. K884.241.11

中国国家版本馆CIP数据核字第2024HB5321号

京审字（2024）G 第1422号

豫见东非 中肯考古

——博戈里亚湖遗址石制品研究

编　　者　河南省文物考古研究院
　　　　　洛阳市考古研究院
　　　　　肯尼亚国家博物馆

责任编辑　孙　丹
责任印制　张　丽

出版发行　文物出版社
社　　址　北京市东城区东直门内北小街2号楼
邮　　编　100007
网　　址　http://www.wenwu.com
邮　　箱　wenwu1957@126.com
经　　销　新华书店
制版印刷　天津裕同印刷有限公司
开　　本　889mm×1194mm　1/16
印　　张　19
版　　次　2024年10月第1版
印　　次　2024年10月第1次印刷
书　　号　ISBN 978-7-5010-8525-5
定　　价　420.00元

编委会

EDITORIAL COMMITTEE

目 录

CONTENTS

序

人类起源和现代人起源是考古学中最重要的国际前沿课题。在考古学研究领域，古人类、旧石器时代占人类历史（约 300 万年）百分之九十九以上，旧石器时代考古在世界范围内使用相同的方法和术语，解决相同的学术问题，吸引了不同国家学者们的目光。肯尼亚是人类发源地之一，也是“现代人非洲起源说”的重要地区。

在中非合作论坛机制和“一带一路”倡议的推动下，2014 年河南省文物局与肯尼亚国家博物馆签订合作框架协议，在此基础上，2017 年河南省文物考古研究院与肯尼亚国家博物馆首次签订合作发掘协议。2017—2018 年，由河南省文物考古研究院、山东大学、洛阳市考古研究院和肯尼亚国家博物馆组成的联合考古队，发掘吉门基石遗址并在周边开展旧石器考古调查。2019、2023 年，河南省文物考古研究院、洛阳市考古研究院与肯尼亚国家博物馆组成联合考古队，发现并发掘了博戈里亚湖遗址第 1 、第 2 和第 3 地点，发掘面积 143 平方米。

中肯旧石器联合考古项目主要以东非肯尼亚巴林戈湖、博戈里亚湖周边零星的旧石器时代中期遗址为线索，寻找更多距今 30 万—10 万年之间的旧石器时代中期遗址，完善巴林戈湖、博戈里亚湖旧石器遗址群的文化序列；在系统发掘后对出土的旧石器遗存进行全面深入研究，将其与河南地区以许昌人遗址、汝州温泉遗址、鲁山仙人洞遗址为代表的旧石器时代中晚期遗址进行对比研究，为中国现代人起源研究寻找新的线索和证据，争取为解决现代人起源等世界前沿课题作出贡献。目前，考古工作仍处于初始阶段，由于种种原因，实际野外工作时间总时长不足 7 个月，想要真正解决现代人起源等重要学术问题，这些工作量是远远不够的。想要有重要发现，必须长期坚持在考古一线，深耕区域性调查、发掘与研究工作。

中肯旧石器联合考古项目得到国家文物局、中国驻肯尼亚大使馆的大力支持，至今已开展四年。中国考古学者西行东非，探索现代人起源的奥秘，天时地利，恰逢其时，为推动共建“一带一路”高质量发展贡献河南智慧，有力推进中肯文明交流互鉴。

河南省文物考古研究院　院长、研究员

2024 年 2 月 10 日

PREFACE

The investigation into the origins and dispersion of early humans and the emergence of Homo sapiens, represents a pivotal and progressive frontier in archaeological research. Paleolithic archaeology, in particular, is of immense significance as it encompasses over 99% of human history, approximately three million years. This discipline is distinguished by its application of standardized methodologies and terminologies on a global scale, addressing universal academic inquiries and garnering the attention of researchers and scholars from a multitude of countries. The Republic of Kenya, situated in East Africa, is acknowledged as one of the cradles of early humankind and plays a crucial role in the research concerning the origins of modern humans.

Under the auspices of the Forum on China-Africa Cooperation (FOCAC) and the promotion of the Belt and Road Initiative, the Henan Provincial Administration of Cultural Heritage conducted the Sino-Kenya Paleolithic Archaeological Project. In 2014, a cooperation framework agreement was formalized between the Henan Provincial Administration of Cultural Heritage and the National Museums of Kenya. Building upon this foundation, a cooperative excavation agreement was signed in 2017 between the Henan Provincial Institute of Cultural Heritage and Archaeology and the National Museums of Kenya. From 2017 to 2018, a joint archaeological team comprising members from the Henan Provincial Institute of Cultural Heritage and Archaeology, Shandong University, Luoyang City Cultural Relics and Archaeology Research Institute, and the National Museums of Kenya excavated the Kimengich Site and conducted extensive surveys on Paleolithic sites in the surrounding areas. In 2019 and 2023, a joint archaeological team consisting of the Henan Provincial Institute of Cultural Heritage and Archaeology, the Luoyang City Cultural Relics and Archaeology Research Institute, and the National Museums of Kenya discovered and excavated three localities with a total area of 143 square meters at the Lake Bogoria site.

The Sino-Kenya Paleolithic Archaeological Project is dedicated to discovering new sites of the Middle Paleolithic period located around Lake Baringo and Lake Bogoria in Kenya, which date back between 300,000 and 100,000 years. The primary objective of the project is to conduct a thorough analysis of the Paleolithic remains discovered in these regions and to compare them with Middle and Late Paleolithic sites in Henan, such as the Xuchang Man Site, the Ruzhou Wenquan Site and the Lushan Xianrendong Site. Through this comparative study, the project further seeks to contribute to the understanding of the origins of modern humans both in China and in other parts of the world. However, due to various constraints, the total duration of the fieldwork has been limited to less than seven months. This insufficient timeframe highlights the necessity for continued regional surveys, excavations, and research to achieve a comprehensive understanding of the origins of modern humans and other significant scientific inquiries. Ongoing efforts in these areas are crucial for making substantial discoveries and advancing our knowledge of human prehistory.

The Sino-Kenya Paleolithic Archaeological Project, supported by National Cultural Heritage Administration of China and the Chinese Embassy in Kenya, has been ongoing for the past four years. Chinese archaeologists are travelling to East Africa to explore the mystery of the origins of modern man, which is a perfect timing to contribute to the wisdom of Henan for the promotion of high-quality development of the Belt and Road Initiative. Additionally, this expedition will significantly enhance cultural exchanges and mutual understanding between China and Kenya.

Director and senior researcher of Henan Provincial Institute
of Cultural Heritage and Archaeology

Liu Haiwang
February 10, 2024

序

当我为这本记录中肯旧石器联合考古项目成果的图录撰写序言时，我的心情无比激动。这不仅是因为此次跨国考古合作所取得的显著成就，更是因为它体现了中非文化交流合作的深远意义和“一带一路”倡议的人文精神。

在中非合作论坛机制的推动下，河南省文物考古研究院与肯尼亚国家博物馆等实施了中肯旧石器联合考古项目，至今已开展四年，推进了中肯两国文明交流互鉴。

首先，我要向河南省文物局、河南省文物考古研究院、山东大学、洛阳市考古研究院以及肯尼亚国家博物馆等机构及其工作人员表达深深的敬意和感谢。是他们的辛勤努力，让这次国际合作成为可能，并取得了丰富的学术成果。通过他们的双手，我们得以一窥远古人类的生活面貌，我们对旧石器时代中期，特别是距今 30 万—10 万年间古人类活动的理解得以深化。这本书的内容对考古学学生和专业人士以及古人类爱好者都是宝贵的资源。也许这本书会激励新的一代古生物学家，他们将深入挖掘并揭示人类在非洲的根源和相互联系。中国与肯尼亚虽远隔万里，但共同的考古追求和对知识探索的渴望，使我们跨越地域和文化的界限携手合作。这种合作不仅促进了两国之间的文化交流，也为国际学术界带来了新的研究视角和发现。中肯双方考古人员在技术和理念上达成共识，共同克服困难，展示了科学探索无国界的精神。

值得一提的是，2024 年 1 月 30 日，由中国社会科学院主办的考古学论坛将博戈里亚湖遗址评为“2023 年国外考古新发现”，这是对中肯考古团队工作的极大肯定。这一成就不仅彰显了考古团队的专业水平和敬业精神，也证明了中非合作在人文领域的巨大潜力和广阔前景。

展望未来，我相信随着“一带一路”建设的不断推进和中非合作的日益深化，中肯两国在考古领域的合作将会取得更多丰硕的成果，为我们带来更多关于人类起源和文明进程的知识。这不仅是对历史的探索，也是对未来的启迪。

最后，我希望这本书能够激发广大读者对古人类历史和考古科学的兴趣，也希望它能成为中肯友好合作的象征，激励我们继续在探索人类起源这一伟大课题上不懈努力。

谨以此序，祝愿中肯旧石器联合考古项目取得更多成就，也祝愿中肯友谊长存，历久弥坚。

肯尼亚国家博物馆　馆长

玛丽 · 吉昆古

2024 年 2 月 15 日

PREFACE

I am incredibly excited as I write the preface for this pictorial record of the achievements of the Sino-Kenya Paleolithic Archaeological Project. This excitement stems not only from the significant accomplishments of this international archaeological collaboration but also from its profound significance in showcasing the cultural exchange and cooperation under the Belt and Road Initiative between China and Africa.

Under the auspices of the Forum on China-Africa Cooperation, the Sino-Kenya Paleolithic Archaeological Project, implemented by the Henan Provincial Institute of Cultural Heritage and Archaeology, Shandong University, Luoyang City Cultural Relics and Archaeology Research Institute, and the National Museums of Kenya, has been ongoing for four years. This project has greatly advanced cultural exchanges and mutual learning between China and Kenya.

First and foremost, I extend my deepest respect and gratitude to the Henan Provincial Administration of Cultural Heritage, the Henan Provincial Institute of Cultural Heritage and Archaeology, Shandong University, Luoyang City Cultural Relics and Archaeology Research Institute, the National Museums of Kenya, and all the personnel involved. It is their hard work and dedication that made this international collaboration possible and yielded rich academic results. Through their efforts, we have glimpsed into the lives of ancient humans and deepened our understanding of human activities during the Middle Paleolithic period, particularly between 300,000 and 100,000 years ago. The contents of this book are a valuable resource for archaeology students and professionals as well as human evolution enthusiasts. Perhaps this book will inspire a new generation of paleontologists who will dig deeper and unravel humanity's interconnectedness and its deepest roots in Africa. Despite the geographical and cultural distances between China and Kenya, our shared pursuit of archaeology and thirst for knowledge have transcended boundaries, fostering cooperation. This collaboration not only promotes cultural exchanges between the two countries but also brings new research perspectives and discoveries to the international academic community. Archaeologists from China and Kenya have reached consensus in terms of technology and ideas, overcome difficulties together, and demonstrated the spirit of borderless scientific exploration.

It is worth mentioning that on January 30, 2024, the Archaeological Forum hosted by the Chinese Academy of Social Sciences awarded the Lake Bogoria Site the title of "2023 Overseas New Archaeological Discovery," which is a great affirmation of the work of the Sino-Kenya archaeological team. This achievement not only highlights the professionalism and dedication of the archaeological team but also proves the immense potential and broad prospects of China-Africa cooperation in the field of humanities.

Looking ahead, I believe that with the continuous advancement of the Belt and Road Initiative and the deepening of China-Africa cooperation, the cooperation between China and Kenya in the field of archaeology will achieve more fruitful results, bringing us more knowledge about human origins and civilization processes. This is not only an exploration of history but also an inspiration for the future.

In conclusion, I hope that this pictorial record will inspire readers' interest in the history of ancient humans and archaeology. I also hope it will serve as a symbol of friendly cooperation between China and Kenya, inspiring us to continue our relentless efforts in exploring the great topic of human origins.

With this preface, I wish the Sino-Kenya Paleolithic Archaeological Project continued success and everlasting friendship between China and Kenya.

Professor and Director of National Museums of Kenya

February 15, 2024

I

The Lake Bogoria Site is located in Marigat Town, Baringo County, Rift Valley Province, Kenya. Its geographic coordinates are N 0° 26'57.83", E 35° 58'56.21", at an altitude of 1015 meters. Situated between Lake Bogoria and Lake Baringo, it is 12 km northeast of Lake Baringo, 15km southeast of Lake Bogoria, and 13 km northwest of the Kimengich Site. The area is characterized by a dense network of rivers that feed into Lake Baringo and Lake Bogoria. The site is bordered by low hills to the west and a lakeshore plain to the east, featuring an eroded landscape with Quaternary sediments and sparse surface vegetation. Rainwater erosion has exposed a significant number of lithic products and animal fossils on the surface, indicating a rich cultural deposit. Preliminary studies have identified remains from the Early, Middle, and Late Paleolithic period at the Lake Bogoria site. Notably, the stone artifacts produced by Levallois technology provide crucial materials for investigating their origins and their relationship with early modern humans.

LAKE BOGORIA SITE OVERVIEW

壹 工作概况

博戈里亚湖遗址（Lake Bogoria Site）位于肯尼亚裂谷省巴林戈郡马里加特镇，地理坐标为北纬 0° 26'57.83"，东经 35° 58'56.21"，海拔 1015 米。地处东非大裂谷博戈里亚湖与巴林戈湖之间，东北距巴林戈湖 12 千米，东南距博戈里亚湖 15 千米，西北距吉门基石遗址 13 千米。遗址周边河流密布，分别汇入巴林戈湖和博戈里亚湖，遗址西边为低山丘陵，东边为湖滨平原。遗址为侵蚀地貌，地表为第四纪沉积物，植被较少。经雨水冲刷，大量石制品、动物化石等在地表上暴露，表明此处堆积十分丰富。初步研究表明，博戈里亚湖遗址包含旧石器时代早、中、晚三期遗存，发现的勒瓦娄哇技术制作的石制品为探讨其起源及其与早期现代人的关系提供了重要材料。

博戈里亚湖遗址航拍图（由西向东）
Aerial photo of the Lake Bogoria Site (from west to east)

博戈里亚湖
Lake Bogoria
第 2 地点
Locality 2
第 1 地点
Locality 1

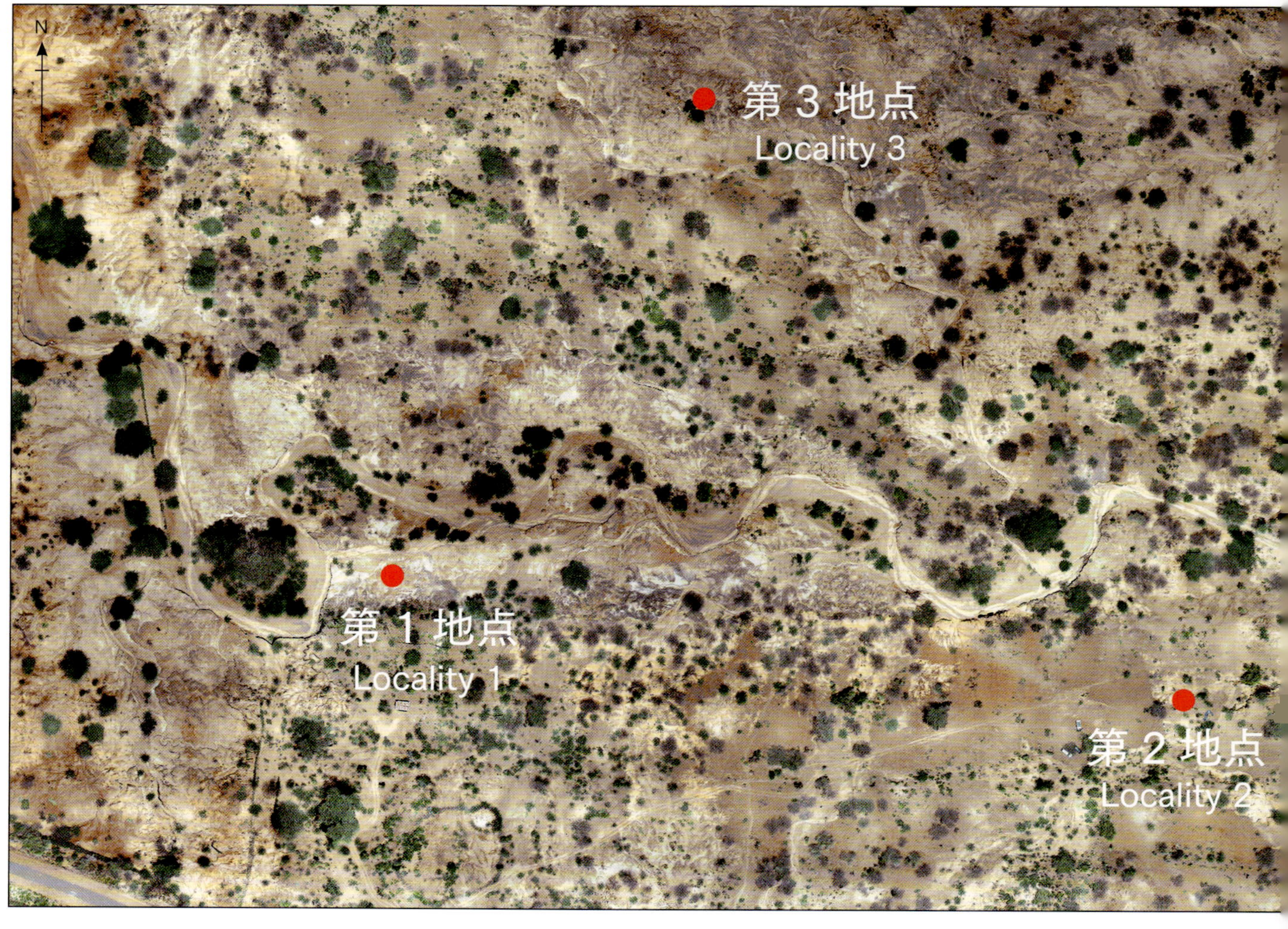

博戈里亚湖遗址航拍图
Aerial photo of the Lake Bogoria Site

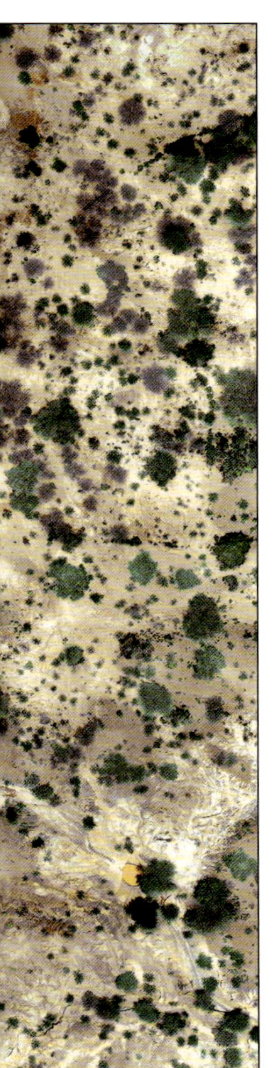

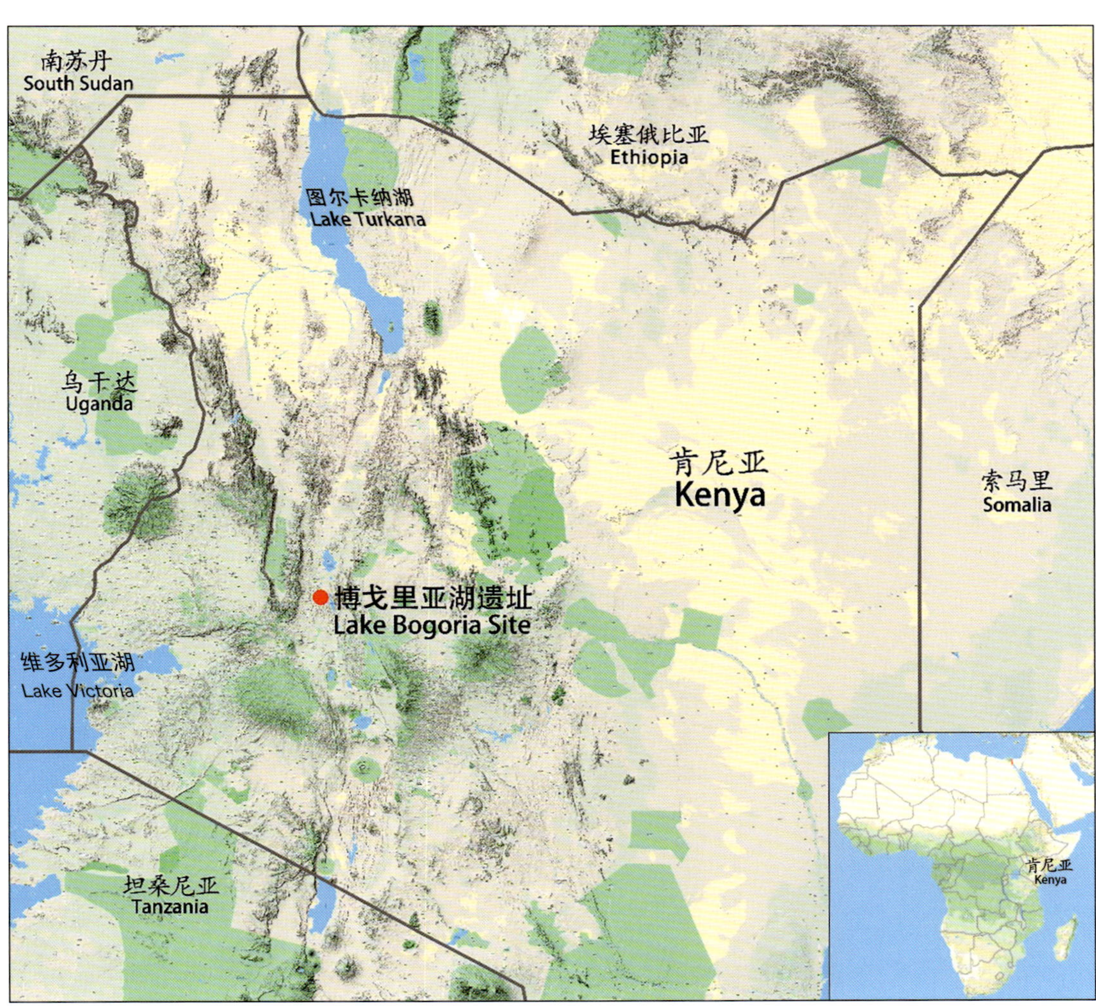

博戈里亚湖遗址地理位置示意图
Geographic location of the Lake Bogoria Site

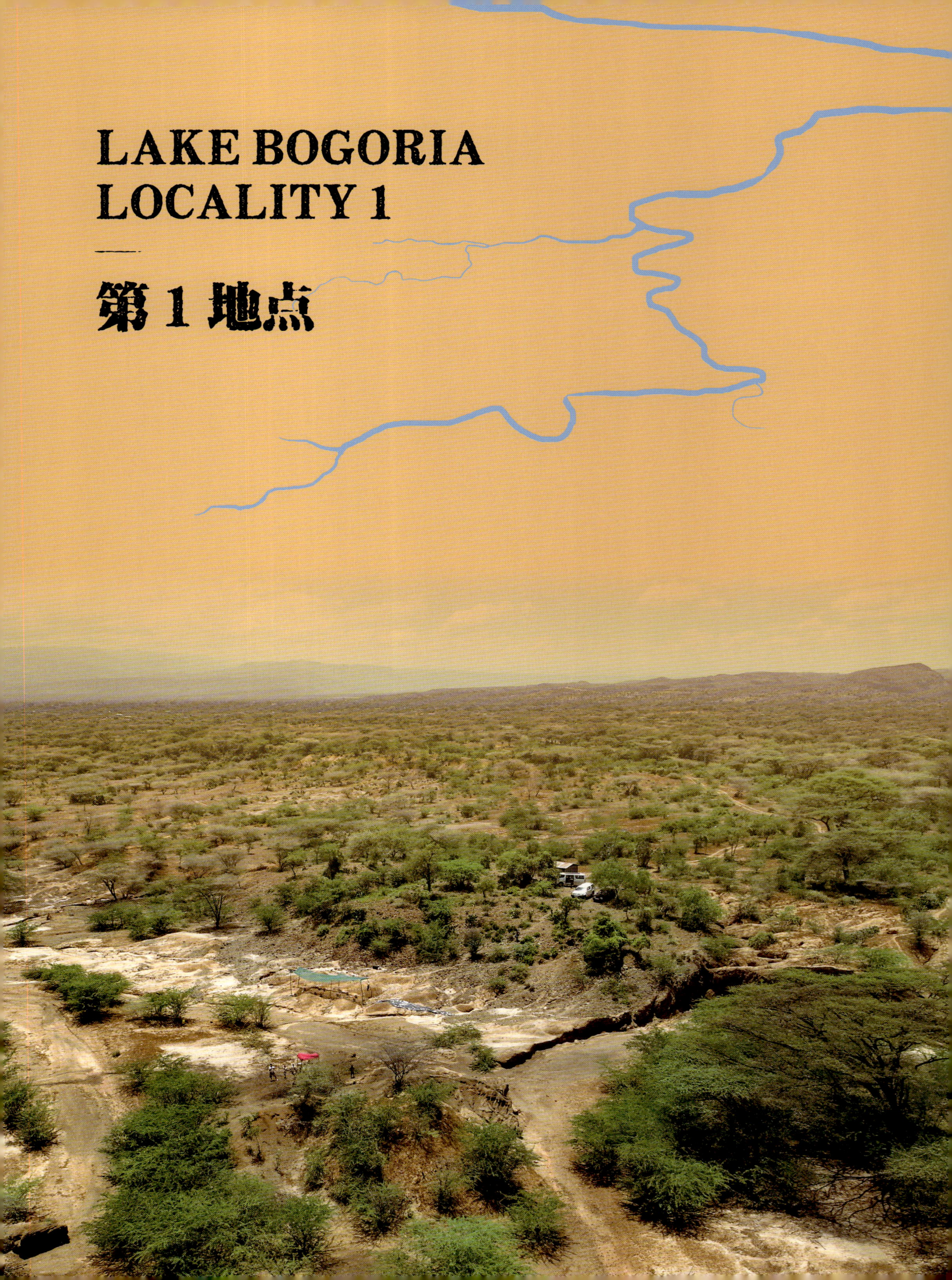
LAKE BOGORIA
LOCALITY 1
第 1 地点

1. 博戈里亚湖第 1 地点航拍图（2019 年）
Aerial photo of the Lake Bogoria Locality 1 (2019)

2. 博戈里亚湖第 1 地点（2019 年）
The Lake Bogoria Locality 1 (2019)

3. 在博戈里亚湖第 1 地点架设全站仪（2019 年）
Setting up the total station at the Lake Bogoria Locality 1 (2019)

4. 博戈里亚湖第 1 地点：过筛（2019 年）
Soil screening at Locality 1 (2019)

5. 博戈里亚湖第 1 地点发掘现场（2019 年）
Excavation area of Locality 1 (2019)

6. 博戈里亚湖第 1 地点：午餐（2019 年）
Having lunch at Locality 1 (2019)

7. 博戈里亚湖第 1 地点发掘结束（2019 年）
The end of excavation of Locality 1 (2019)

8
9

8. 博戈里亚湖遗址第 1 地点发掘结束（2019 年）
The end of excavation of Locality 1 (2019)

9. 中肯旧石器联合考古队合影（2019 年）
The photo of Sino-Kenya Paleolithic Archaeological Team (2019)

博高利亚湖遗址
Lake Bogoria Site
中肯旧石器联合考古
Sino-Kenya Paleolithic Archaeological Project
Henan Provincial Institute of
Cultural Heritage and Archaeology

LAKE BOGORIA
LOCALITY 2
第 2 地点

1. 博戈里亚湖第 2 地点航拍图（2019 年）
Aerial photo of the Lake Bogoria Locality 2 (2019)

2. 博戈里亚湖第 2 地点航拍图（2019 年）
Aerial photo of the Lake Bogoria Locality 2 (2019)

3. 标记第 2 地点地表遗物（2019 年）
Marking lithics discovered from the surface of the Lake Bogoria Locality 2 (2019)

4. 测量、采集第 2 地点地表遗物（2019 年）
Measuring and collecting lithics found from the surface of Locality 2 (2019)

5. 博戈里亚湖第 2 地点布方示意图
Schematic diagram of grid system of Locality 2

N

P3 M3 L3 I3 H3 E3 D3 A3
P2 M2 L2 I2 H2 E2 D2 A2
Q1 P1 M1 L1 I1 H1 E1 D1 A1
T Q P M L I H E D A
S R O N K J G F C B
S1 R1 O1 N1 K1 J1 G1 F1 C1 B1

红色系为 2023 年发掘
Red tones: Excavated in 2023

灰色系为 2019 年发掘
Grey tones: Excavated in 2019

6. 博戈里亚湖第 2 地点发掘（2019 年）
The excavation of the Lake Bogoria Locality 2 (2019)

7. 第 2 地点探方 U、X 第 1 操作层出土石制品（2019 年）
Stone artifacts unearthed from the first operation layer of Square U and X at Locality 2 (2019)

8
9

8. 第 2 地点探方 U、X、U1、X1 第 2 操作层出土石制品（2019 年）
Stone artifacts unearthed from the 2nd operation layer of Square U, X, U1 and X1 at Locality 2 (2019)

9. 第 2 地点第 2 操作层发掘现场（2019 年）
Excavation area of the 2nd operation layer at Locality 2 (2019)

10 | 11
12

10. 商讨第 2 地点发掘方案（2023 年）
Discussing the excavation plan of Locality 2 (2023)

11. 在第 2 地点架设 RTK（2023 年）
Setting up RTK at Locality 2 (2023)

12. 第 2 地点发掘现场（2023 年）
Excavation area of Locality 2 (2023)

13. 第 2 地点出土的勒瓦娄哇尖状器（2023 年）
Levallois point unearthed from Locality 2 (2023)

14. 第 2 地点发掘结束（2023 年）
The end of excavation of Locality 2 (2023)

15. 第 2 地点发掘结束考古队员合影（2023 年）
The photo of the archaeological team at the end of excavation at Locality 2 (2023)

13 | 14 / 15

16 | 17 | 18

16. 督导团赴博戈里亚湖第 2 地点指导工作（2019 年）
The steering group at Locality 2 (2019)

17. 督导团赴博戈里亚湖第 2 地点指导工作（2023 年）
The steering group at Locality 2 (2023)

18. 中肯旧石器联合考古队合影（2023 年）
The photo of Sino-Kenya Paleolithic Archaeological Team (2023)

SURVEY

调查

1 | 2
  | 3

1. 考古队员野外调查（2019 年）
Archaeological field survey (2019)

2. 考古队员野外调查（2019 年）
Archaeological field survey (2019)

3. 考古队员野外调查（2019 年）
Archaeological field survey (2019)

4. 调查发现的旧石器地点（2019 年）
Paleolithic site discovered during the field survey (2019)

5. 调查发现的地层中的石制品（2019 年）
Stone artifacts in strata discovered during the field survey (2019)

6

7

6. 调查发现的动物化石（2019 年）
Animal fossils discovered during the field survey (2019)

7. 调查发现的石制品（2019 年）
Stone artifacts discovered during the field survey (2019)

8 | 9 | 10

8. 考古队员野外调查（2023 年）
Archaeological field survey (2023)

9. 考古队员野外调查（2023 年）
Archaeological field survey (2023)

10. 考古队员野外调查（2023 年）
Archaeological field survey (2023)

11 | 13
12 |

11. 调查发现的地层中的石制品（2023 年）
Stone artifacts in strata discovered during the field survey (2023)

12. 调查发现的石制品（2023 年）
Stone artifacts discovered during the field survey (2023)

13. 调查发现的旧石器地点（2023 年）
Paleolithic site discovered during the field survey (2023)

14 | 16
15 | 17

14. 调查发现的石制品（2023 年）
Stone artifacts discovered during the field survey (2023)

15. 讨论野外调查发现的石制品（2023 年）
Discussing the stone artifacts discovered during the field survey (2023)

16. 调查发现的第 4 地点（2023 年）
The Lake Bogoria Locality 4 discovered during the field survey (2023)

17. 培训肯方队员使用无人机（2023 年）
Drone training with Kenyan teammates (2023)

18 | 20
19 |

18. 第 3 地点地表石制品（2023 年）
Stone artifacts from the surface at Locality 3 (2023)

19. 第 4 地点的石制品和动物化石（2023 年）
Stone artifacts and animal fossils at Locality 4 (2023)

20. 考古队员受邀到新华社非洲总分社交流座谈
The archaeological team was invited to a symposium at the Africa headquarters of the Xinhua News Agency

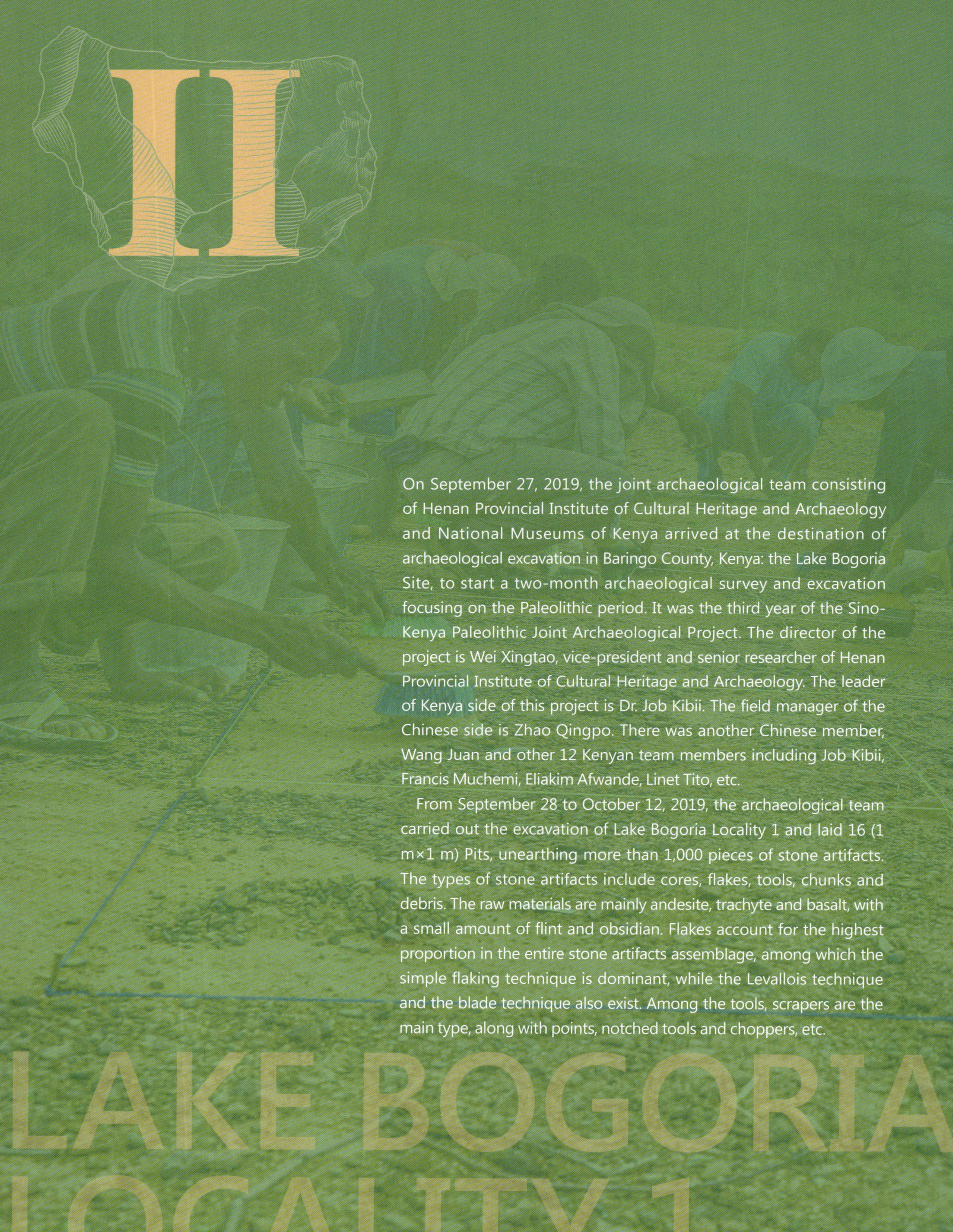

II

On September 27, 2019, the joint archaeological team consisting of Henan Provincial Institute of Cultural Heritage and Archaeology and National Museums of Kenya arrived at the destination of archaeological excavation in Baringo County, Kenya: the Lake Bogoria Site, to start a two-month archaeological survey and excavation focusing on the Paleolithic period. It was the third year of the Sino-Kenya Paleolithic Joint Archaeological Project. The director of the project is Wei Xingtao, vice-president and senior researcher of Henan Provincial Institute of Cultural Heritage and Archaeology. The leader of Kenya side of this project is Dr. Job Kibii. The field manager of the Chinese side is Zhao Qingpo. There was another Chinese member, Wang Juan and other 12 Kenyan team members including Job Kibii, Francis Muchemi, Eliakim Afwande, Linet Tito, etc.

From September 28 to October 12, 2019, the archaeological team carried out the excavation of Lake Bogoria Locality 1 and laid 16 (1 m×1 m) Pits, unearthing more than 1,000 pieces of stone artifacts. The types of stone artifacts include cores, flakes, tools, chunks and debris. The raw materials are mainly andesite, trachyte and basalt, with a small amount of flint and obsidian. Flakes account for the highest proportion in the entire stone artifacts assemblage, among which the simple flaking technique is dominant, while the Levallois technique and the blade technique also exist. Among the tools, scrapers are the main type, along with points, notched tools and choppers, etc.

LAKE BOGORIA LOCALITY 1

第1地点石制品

2019年9月27日，由河南省文物考古研究院和肯尼亚国家博物馆组成的旧石器联合考古队抵达肯尼亚巴林戈郡的考古目的地——博戈里亚湖遗址，开始为期近两个月的旧石器考古调查、发掘工作。这是中肯旧石器联合考古项目实施的第三年。项目主任为河南省文物考古研究院魏兴涛副院长、研究员，肯方项目负责人为Job Kibii，中方现场负责人为赵清坡，中方成员有王娟，肯方成员有Job Kibii、Francis Muchemi、Eliakim Afwande、Linet Tito等12人。2019年9月28日—10月12日，发掘博戈里亚湖第1地点，布1米×1米探方16个，完成发掘面积16平方米，发现石制品1000余件。石制品类型有石核、石片、工具、断块和碎屑，原料以安山岩、粗面岩和玄武岩为主，另有少量燧石和黑曜岩。石片在整个石制品组合中占比最高，其中又以简单剥片技术为主，同时存在勒瓦娄哇技术和石叶技术。工具中则以刮削器为主，同时还有尖状器、凹缺器和砍砸器等。

CORE

石核

石核 core　GoJh14：1174
66 mm × 66 mm × 54 mm

石核 core　GoJh14：1200
27 mm × 23 mm × 30 mm

0 2cm

石核 core

GoJh14：2007
72 mm × 63 mm × 25 mm

石核 core

GoJh14：2332
51 mm × 34 mm × 26 mm

0 1cm

0 2cm

石核 core
GoJh14：2062
60 mm × 54 mm × 34 mm

LEVALLOIS CORE

勒瓦娄哇石核

勒瓦娄哇石核 Levallois core

GoJh14：1671
41 mm × 45 mm × 20 mm

勒瓦娄哇石核 Levallois core

GoJh14：1770
71 mm × 49 mm × 26 mm

FLAKE

石片

石片 GoJh14：646
flake 41 mm × 22 mm × 18 mm

石片 GoJh14：914
flake 53 mm × 32 mm × 12 mm

石片 GoJh14：1237
flake 50 mm × 28 mm × 12 mm

石片 GoJh14：1628
flake 45 mm × 26 mm × 10 mm

石片 flake

GoJh14 ：2019
48 mm × 47 mm × 15 mm

石片 flake

GoJh14 ：2168
34 mm × 22 mm × 8 mm

石片 flake
GoJh14：1112
43 mm × 31 mm × 6 mm

石片 flake
GoJh14：1135
36 mm × 47 mm × 8 mm

石片 flake
GoJh14：1153
14 mm × 16 mm × 3 mm

石片 flake
GoJh14：1355
44 mm × 24 mm × 10 mm

石片 flake
GoJh14：1376
27 mm × 16 mm × 7 mm

石片 flake
GoJh14：1787
27 mm × 18 mm × 5 mm

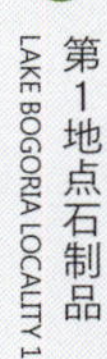

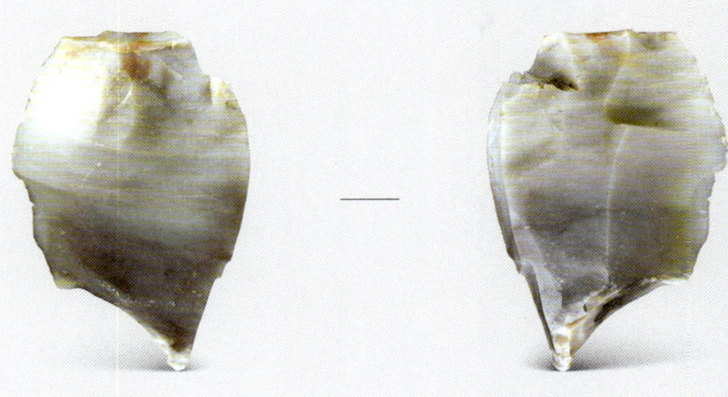

0 2cm

石片 flake

GoJh14：2078
42 mm × 28 mm × 9 mm

0 2cm

石片（远端缺失） flake

GoJh14：500
39 mm × 27 mm × 5 mm

LEVALLOIS FLAKE

勒瓦娄哇石片

勒瓦娄哇石片 GoJh14：538
Levallois flake 51 mm × 25 mm × 8 mm

勒瓦娄哇石片 GoJh14：1122
Levallois flake 57 mm × 56 mm × 13 mm

0 1cm

勒瓦娄哇石片 GoJh14：1649
Levallois flake 36 mm × 22 mm × 7 mm

0 2cm

勒瓦娄哇石片 GoJh14：1705
Levallois flake 51 mm × 33 mm × 5 mm

0 2cm

勒瓦娄哇石片
Levallois flake

GoJh14：2103
64 mm × 35 mm × 12 mm

BLADE

石叶

0 1cm

石叶 GoJh14：503
blade 36 mm × 16 mm × 7 mm

0 2cm

石叶 GoJh14：570
blade 91 mm × 34 mm × 15 mm

石叶 blade

GoJh14：610

49 mm × 19 mm × 7 mm

石叶 blade

GoJh14：678

42 mm × 12 mm × 6 mm

0 2cm

石叶
blade

GoJh14：984
40 mm × 20 mm × 6 mm

0 1cm

石叶
blade

GoJh14：1164
43 mm × 17 mm × 7 mm

石叶
blade

GoJh14：1307
41 mm × 17 mm × 6 mm

石叶
blade

GoJh14：1188
69 mm × 28 mm × 11 mm

0 1cm

石叶 GoJh14：1334
blade 47 mm × 23 mm × 6 mm

0 1cm

石叶 GoJh14：1391
blade 39 mm × 16 mm × 7 mm

石叶 GoJh14：1677
blade 80 mm × 24 mm × 16 mm

石叶 blade
GoJh14：2013
41 mm × 18 mm × 5 mm

石叶（近端） blade
GoJh14：2017
32 mm × 21 mm × 8 mm

0 2cm

石叶 GoJh14 ： 2072
blade 48 mm × 20 mm × 7 mm

0 1cm

石叶 GoJh14 ： 2075
blade 66 mm × 25 mm × 8 mm

石叶 GoJh14 ： 2095
blade 43 mm × 21 mm × 6 mm

石叶 GoJh14 ： 2307
blade 41 mm × 16 mm × 5 mm

石叶 GoJh14 ：2166
blade 41 mm × 19 mm × 9 mm

石叶 GoJh14 ：2328
blade 44 mm × 15 mm × 7 mm

LEVALLOIS BLADE

——

勒瓦娄哇石叶

勒瓦娄哇石叶
Levallois blade

GoJh14 ： 544
54 mm × 26 mm × 7 mm

勒瓦娄哇石叶
Levallois blade

GoJh14 ： 909
65 mm × 24 mm × 11 mm

勒瓦娄哇石叶
Levallois blade
GoJh14：962
42 mm × 21 mm × 10 mm

勒瓦娄哇石叶
Levallois blade
GoJh14：1323
59 mm × 20 mm × 9 mm

勒瓦娄哇石叶 Levallois blade
GoJh14：2182
50 mm × 22 mm × 7 mm

勒瓦娄哇石叶 Levallois blade
GoJh14：2310
47 mm × 19 mm × 10 mm

SCRAPER

刮削器

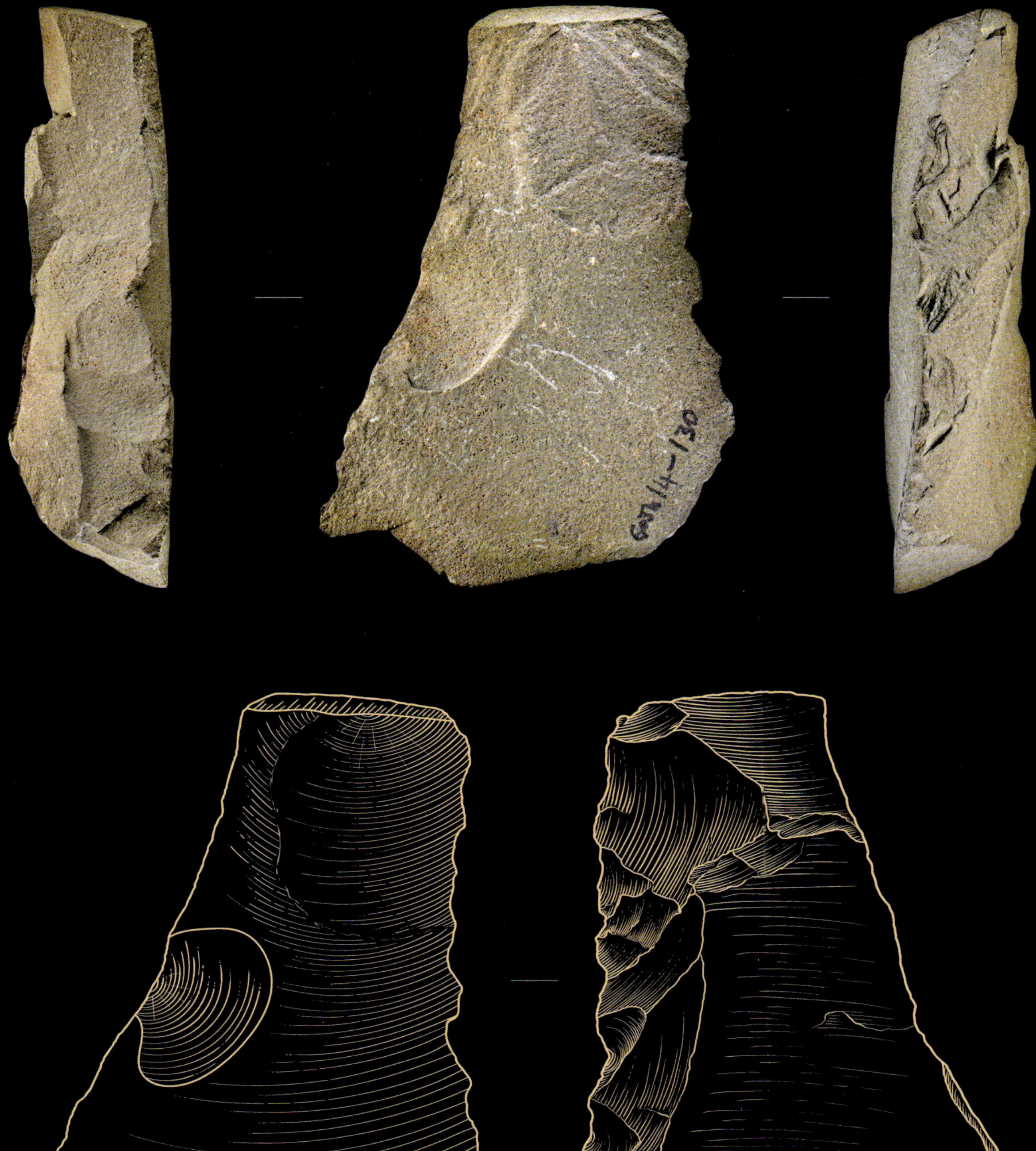

0 2cm

刮削器 scraper ╲ GoJh14：130
91 mm × 61 mm × 24 mm

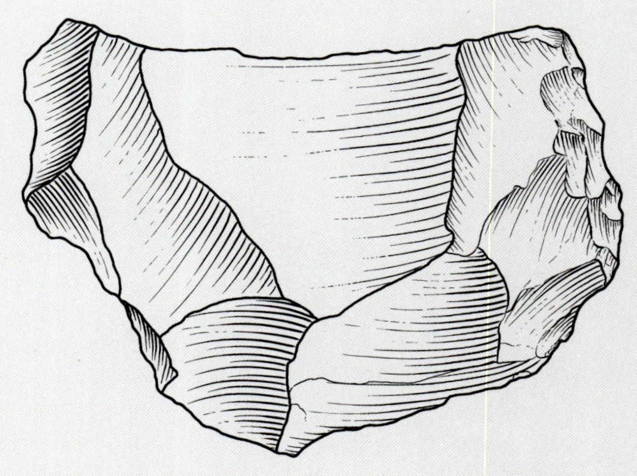

0 1cm

刮削器
scraper

GoJh14：138
40 mm × 33 mm × 13 mm

0 1cm

刮削器 scraper

GoJh14 ： 562
23 mm × 12 mm × 3 mm

0 1cm

刮削器 scraper

GoJh14 ： 580
24 mm × 23 mm × 4 mm

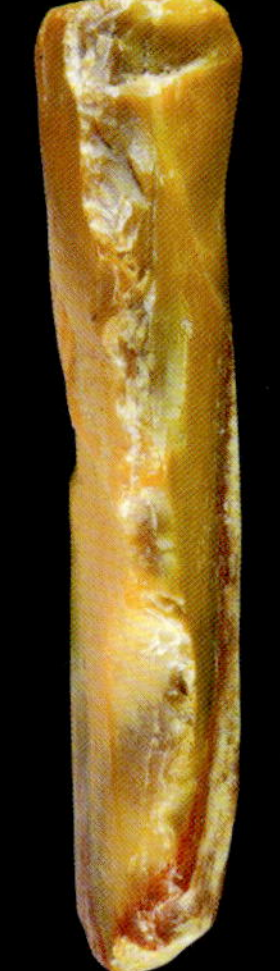

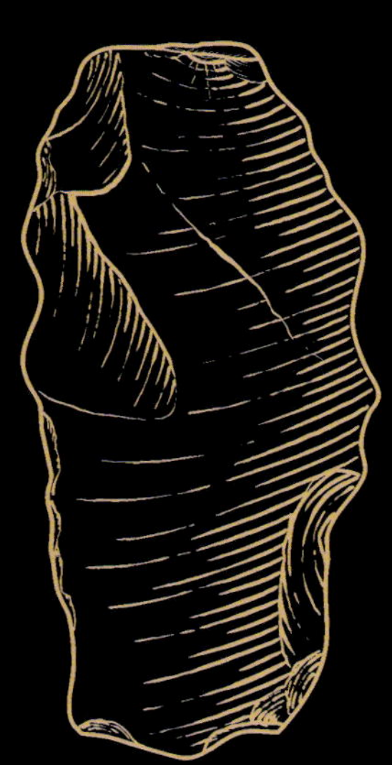

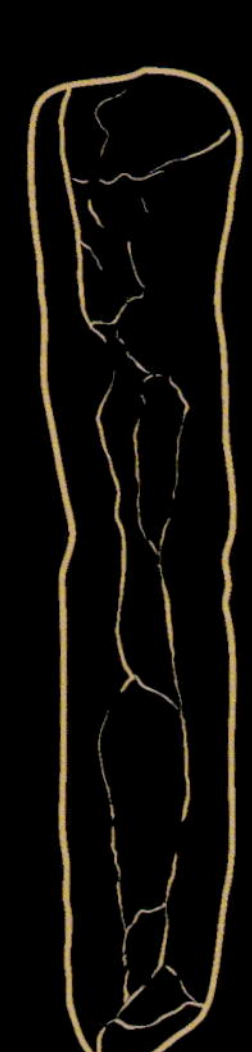

0 2cm

刮削器 scraper

GoJh14：1159
68 mm × 33 mm × 12 mm

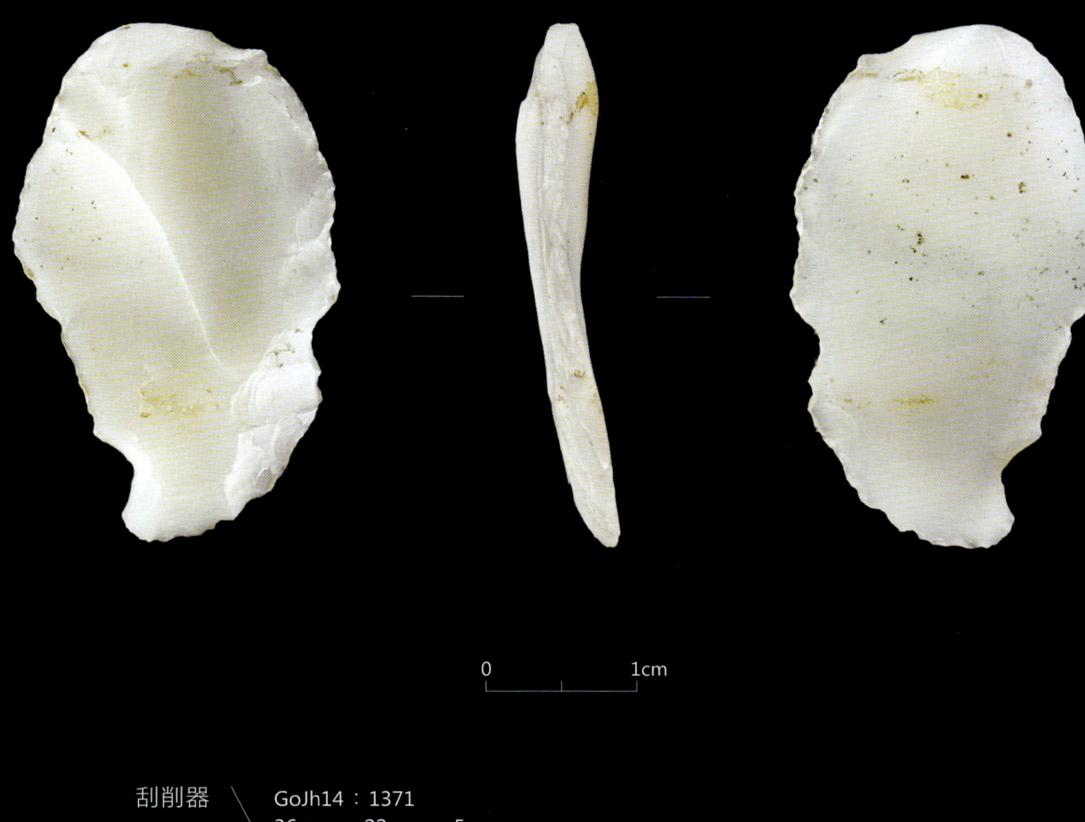

刮削器 scraper
GoJh14：1371
36 mm × 22 mm × 5 mm

刮削器 scraper
GoJh14：1684
18 mm × 16 mm × 4 mm

0 1cm

刮削器 GoJh14：1678
scraper 108 mm × 38 mm × 11 mm

刮削器 scraper GoJh14 ： 1682
39 mm × 20 mm × 6 mm

刮削器 scraper GoJh14 ： 1320
28 mm × 10 mm × 6 mm

刮削器 scraper GoJh14 ： 1274
23 mm × 16 mm × 6 mm

NOTCH

凹缺器

0 1cm

凹缺器 \ GoJh14：1215
notch 30 mm × 25 mm × 9 mm

0 1cm

0 1cm

凹缺器 \ GoJh14：1310
notch 22 mm × 16 mm × 6 mm

凹缺器 \ GoJh14：1201
notch 50 mm × 40 mm × 17 mm

OTHER STONE ARTIFACTS

其他

小石叶
bladelet

GoJh14：1748
35 mm × 11 mm × 3 mm

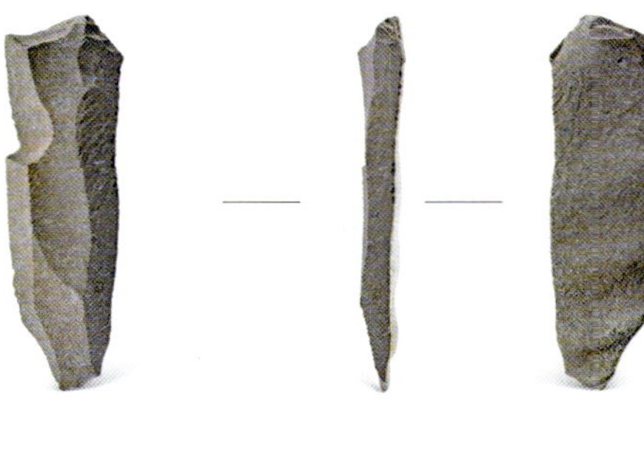

0 2cm

0 2cm

削片
spall

GoJh14：2337
124 mm × 54 mm × 33 mm

0 1cm

尖状器
point

GoJh14 : 543
32 mm × 20 mm × 7 mm

0 2cm

尖状器
point

GoJh14 : 2068
45 mm × 22 mm × 8 mm

勒瓦娄哇尖状器
Levallois point

GoJh14 ： 507
44 mm × 30 mm × 6 mm

勒瓦娄哇尖状器
Levallois point

GoJh14 ： 2167
39 mm × 20 mm × 7 mm

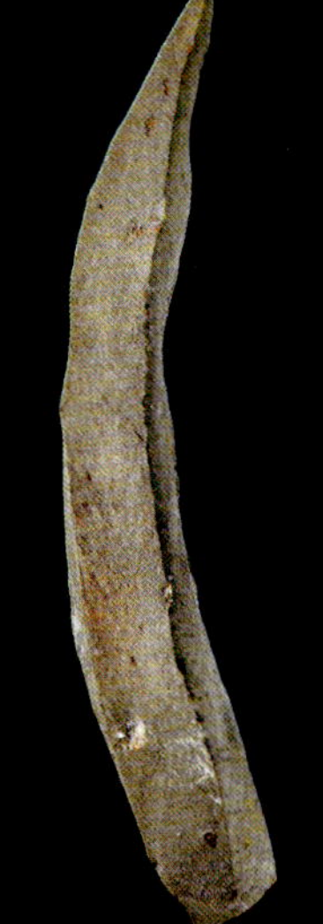

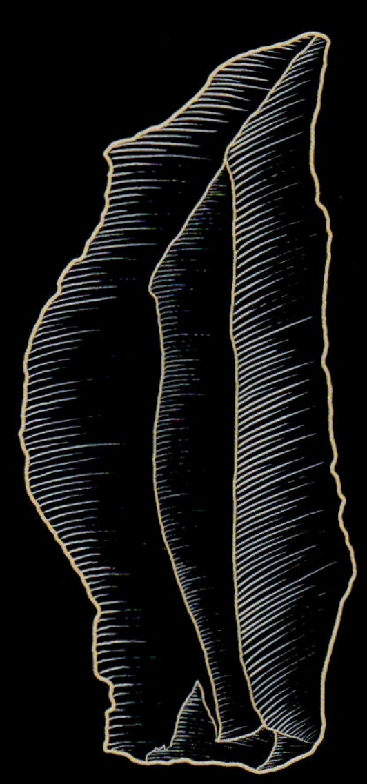
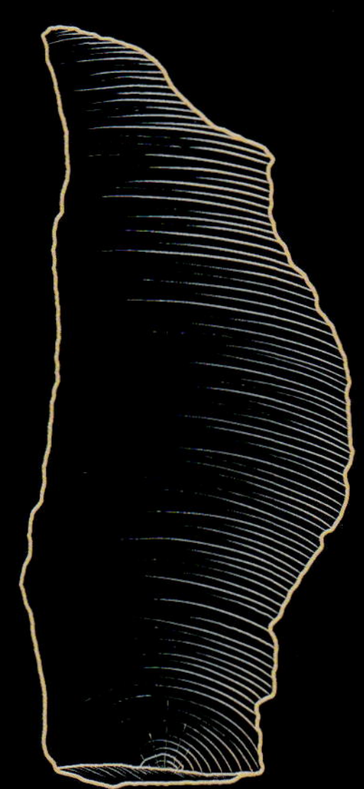

0 2cm

勒瓦娄哇尖状器 Levallois point
GoJh14：1367
74 mm × 31 mm × 12 mm

0 2cm

砍砸器 chopper

GoJh14：2008
75 mm × 85 mm × 57 mm

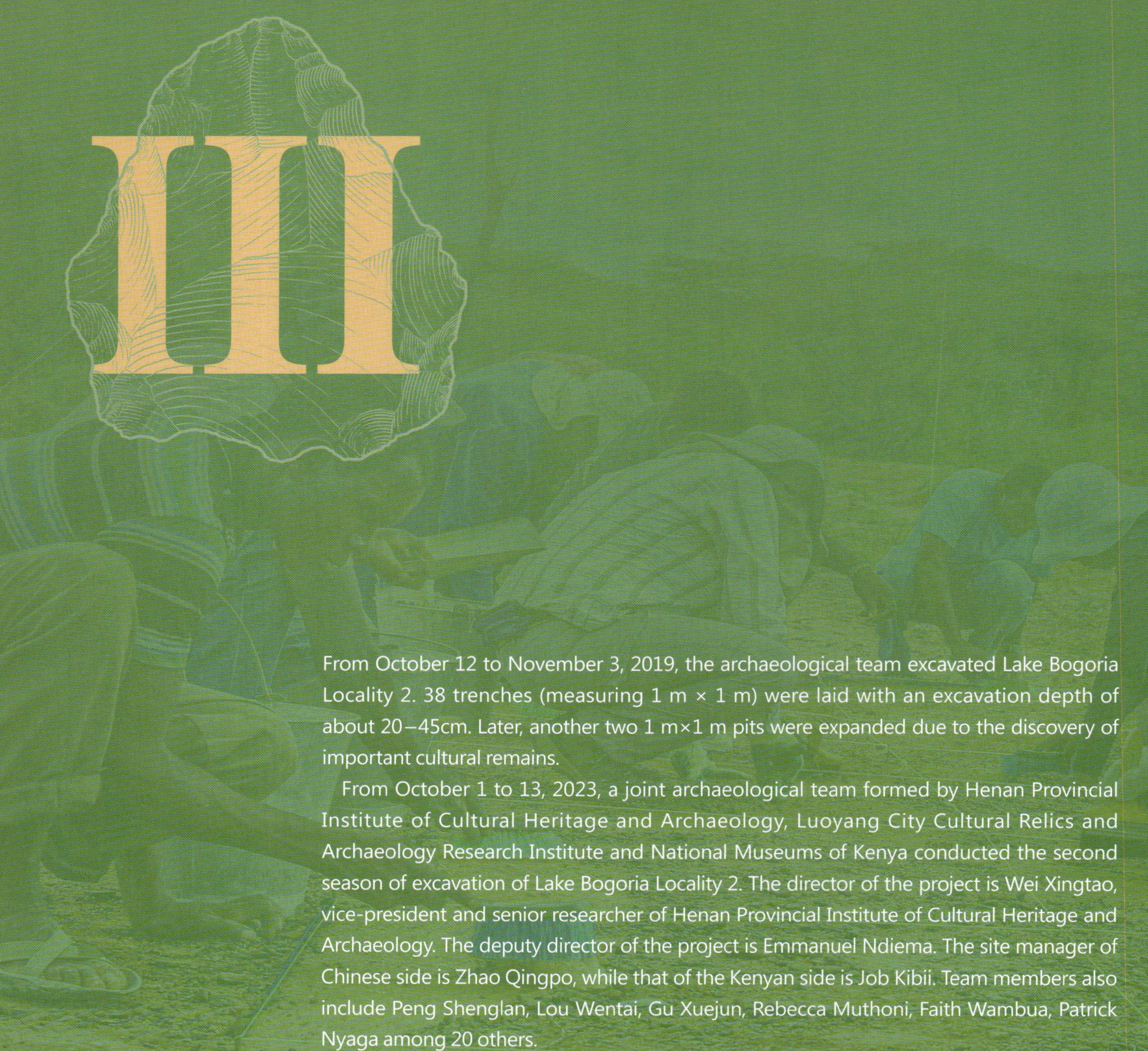

III

From October 12 to November 3, 2019, the archaeological team excavated Lake Bogoria Locality 2. 38 trenches (measuring 1 m × 1 m) were laid with an excavation depth of about 20–45cm. Later, another two 1 m×1 m pits were expanded due to the discovery of important cultural remains.

From October 1 to 13, 2023, a joint archaeological team formed by Henan Provincial Institute of Cultural Heritage and Archaeology, Luoyang City Cultural Relics and Archaeology Research Institute and National Museums of Kenya conducted the second season of excavation of Lake Bogoria Locality 2. The director of the project is Wei Xingtao, vice-president and senior researcher of Henan Provincial Institute of Cultural Heritage and Archaeology. The deputy director of the project is Emmanuel Ndiema. The site manager of Chinese side is Zhao Qingpo, while that of the Kenyan side is Job Kibii. Team members also include Peng Shenglan, Lou Wentai, Gu Xuejun, Rebecca Muthoni, Faith Wambua, Patrick Nyaga among 20 others.

Based on the excavation in 2019, 35 additional units (1 m×1 m) were laid at Locality 2 in 2023, with an excavation depth of about 35–46 cm. More than 1,200 pieces of stone artifacts were found, which were mainly discovered from the volcanic ash layer. Andesite, trachyte and basalt are the main raw materials, followed by a small amount of flint and obsidian. The majority of the artifacts are flakes and debris less than 2 cm, while there are also some stone cores and Levallois points. Because of the high proportion of debris (47%), it could be concluded that Locality 2 is a small lithic production workshop, and stone artifacts are probably found in situ.

LAKE BOGORIA LOCALITY 2

第2地点石制品

2019年10月12日—11月3日，发掘博戈里亚湖遗址第2地点，布1米×1米探方38个，后因有重要遗物出土，又扩1米×1米探方2个，完成发掘面积40平方米，发掘深度20—45厘米。

2023年10月1日—13日，河南省文物考古研究院、洛阳市考古研究院和肯尼亚国家博物馆组成联合考古队，发掘博戈里亚湖第2地点。项目主任为河南省文物考古研究院魏兴涛副院长、研究员，项目副主任为Emmanuel Ndiema，中方现场负责人为赵清坡，肯方项目负责人为Job Kibii。中肯双方队员还有彭胜蓝、娄文台、顾雪军、Rebecca Muthoni、Faith Wambua、Patrick Nyaga等20余人。在2019年发掘工作的基础上，2023年在第2地点另外布设35个1米×1米的探方，完成发掘面积35平方米，发掘深度约为35—46厘米。第2地点共发现石制品1200余件，石制品主要出自火山灰层，原料以安山岩、粗面岩、玄武岩为主，有少量燧石和黑曜岩；类型以石片和小于2厘米的碎屑为主，含少量石核和勒瓦娄哇尖状器，其中碎屑比例高达47%——可判断第2地点为一处小型石器加工场，石制品为原地埋藏。

CORE

石核

石核 core GoJh14：1533
15 mm × 12 mm × 10 mm

石核 core GoJh14：1999
38 mm × 58 mm × 43 mm

石核（盘状） core GoJh14：2479
74 mm × 65 mm × 61 mm

LEVALLOIS CORE

勒瓦娄哇石核

勒瓦娄哇石核
Levallois core

GoJh14：1076
77 mm × 69 mm × 40 mm

勒瓦娄哇石核
Levallois core

GoJh14：88
45 mm × 46 mm × 14 mm

勒瓦娄哇石核
Levallois core

GoJh14：1495
81 mm × 73 mm × 22 mm

勒瓦娄哇石核
Levallois core

GoJh14：1588
62 mm × 53 mm × 35 mm

FLAKE

石片

0 2cm

石片 GoJh14：86
flake 59 mm × 49 mm × 17 mm

0 2cm

石片 GoJh14：401
flake 54 mm × 32 mm × 9 mm

石片 flake GoJh14：1032
55 mm × 91 mm × 30 mm

石片 flake GoJh14：1824
106 mm × 67 mm × 20 mm

石片 flake

GoJh14：1572
75 mm × 93 mm × 36 mm

石片 flake

GoJh14：1837
49 mm × 47 mm × 13 mm

石片 flake

GoJh14：1876
61 mm × 47 mm × 14 mm

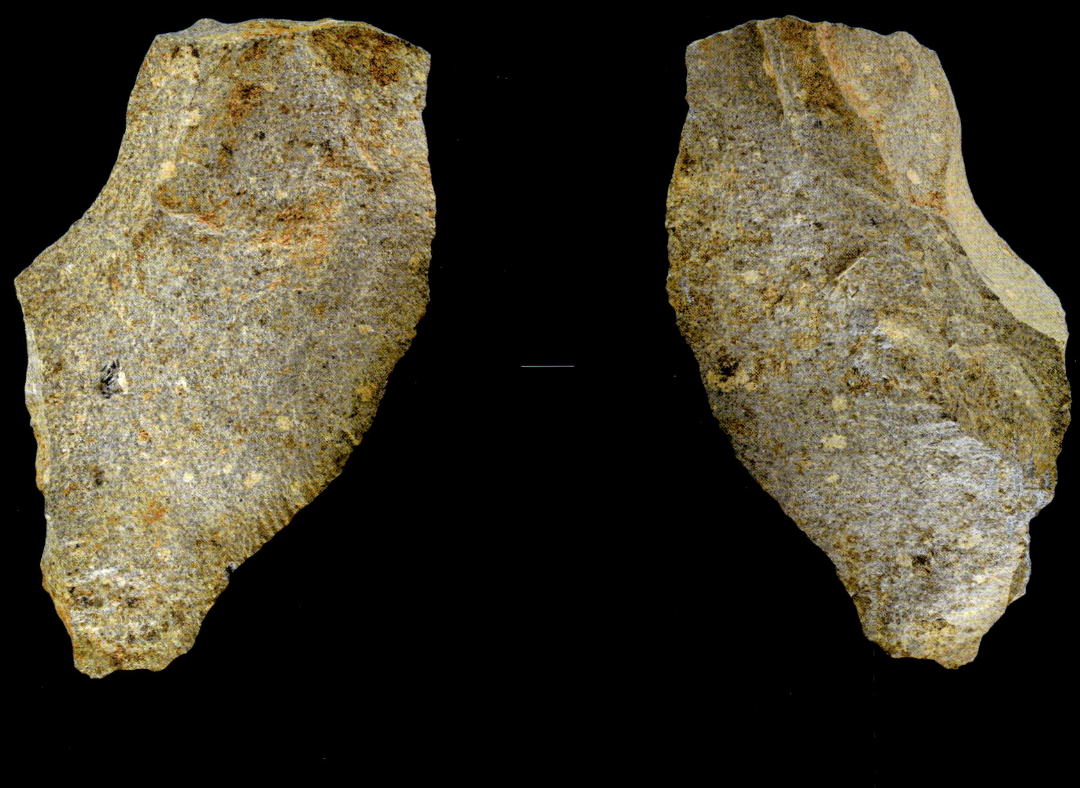

石片 flake

GoJh14：2216
88 mm × 53 mm × 14 mm

0 2cm

石片（右裂片） flake

GoJh14：897
111 mm × 70 mm × 38 mm

0 2cm

石片（左裂片）
flake

GoJh14：1010
66 mm × 56 mm × 17 mm

0 1cm

石片
flake

GoJh14：151
27 mm × 21 mm × 4 mm

石片 GoJh14：179
flake 31 mm × 19 mm × 5 mm

石片 GoJh14：881
flake 27 mm × 22 mm × 6 mm

石片
flake

GoJh14：1095
32 mm × 34 mm × 6 mm

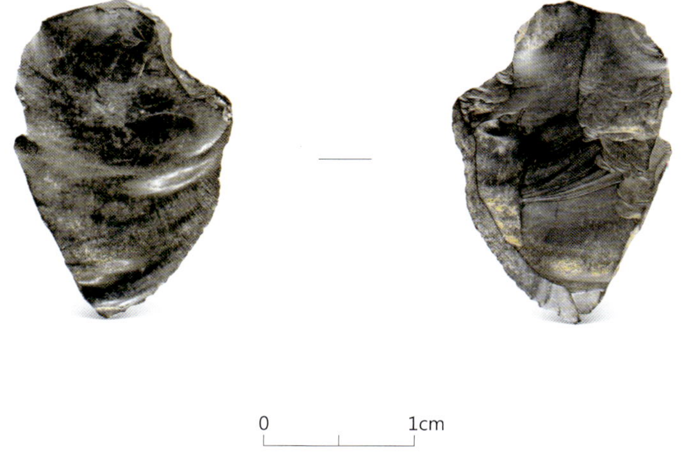

石片
flake

GoJh14：1483
22 mm × 15 mm × 3 mm

石片 flake
GoJh14：1591
42 mm × 38 mm × 13 mm

石片 flake
GoJh14：1846
50 mm × 32 mm × 8 mm

石片 GoJh14：1933
flake 13 mm × 9 mm × 2 mm

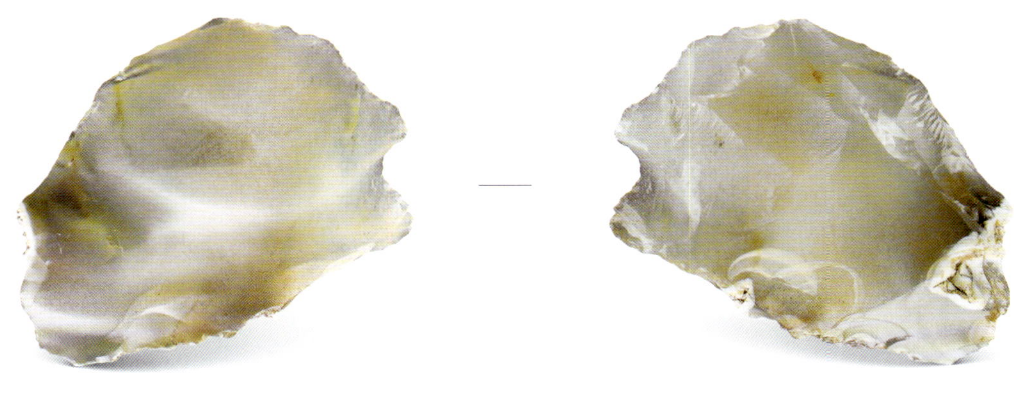

石片 GoJh14：1936
flake 24 mm × 32 mm × 6 mm

石片 GoJh14：2262
flake 45 mm × 28 mm × 8 mm

LEVALLOIS FLAKE

——

勒瓦娄哇石片

勒瓦娄哇石片
Levallois flake

GoJh14：433
88 mm × 50 mm × 16 mm

勒瓦娄哇石片
Levallois flake

GoJh14：442
70 mm × 30 mm × 10 mm

0 2cm

勒瓦娄哇石片
Levallois flake

GoJh14：498
41 mm × 34 mm × 12 mm

0 2cm

勒瓦娄哇石片
Levallois flake

GoJh14：718
36 mm × 23 mm × 4 mm

勒瓦娄哇石片
Levallois flake

GoJh14：753
67 mm × 48 mm × 11 mm

勒瓦娄哇石片
Levallois flake

GoJh14：756
47 mm × 32 mm × 11 mm

勒瓦娄哇石片　GoJh14 ：765
Levallois flake　63 mm × 49 mm × 13 mm

勒瓦娄哇石片　GoJh14 ：780
Levallois flake　52 mm × 39 mm × 9 mm

勒瓦娄哇石片 Levallois flake ╲ GoJh14：846
73 mm × 45 mm × 12 mm

0 2cm

勒瓦娄哇石片 Levallois flake ╲ GoJh14：864
41 mm × 63 mm × 13 mm

勒瓦娄哇石片
Levallois flake

GoJh14：1065
64 mm × 38 mm × 13 mm

0 2cm

勒瓦娄哇石片
Levallois flake

GoJh14：1427
77 mm × 49 mm × 15 mm

0 2cm

勒瓦娄哇石片
Levallois flake

GoJh14：1531
56 mm × 46 mm × 11 mm

0 2cm

勒瓦娄哇石片
Levallois flake

GoJh14：1551
69 mm × 60 mm × 18 mm

勒瓦娄哇石片
Levallois flake

GoJh14 ：1557
86 mm × 60 mm × 18 mm

勒瓦娄哇石片
Levallois flake

GoJh14 ：1579
59 mm × 54 mm × 20 mm

0 2cm

勒瓦娄哇石片 GoJh14 ：1593
Levallois flake 62 mm × 57 mm × 23 mm

0 2cm

勒瓦娄哇石片 GoJh14 ：1825
Levallois flake 71 mm × 73 mm × 21 mm

勒瓦娄哇石片 GoJh14：1875
Levallois flake 63 mm × 40 mm × 8 mm

勒瓦娄哇石片 GoJh14：2400
Levallois flake 61 mm × 40 mm × 10 mm

BLADE

石叶

石叶 blade

GoJh14 : 412
67 mm × 33 mm × 10 mm

石叶 blade

GoJh14 : 746
76 mm × 30 mm × 13 mm

石叶 blade

GoJh14：840
81 mm × 37 mm × 8 mm

石叶 blade

GoJh14：859
51 mm × 17 mm × 6 mm

石叶 blade

GoJh14：870
33 mm × 14 mm × 5 mm

石叶 blade

GoJh14：1443
83 mm × 41 mm × 16 mm

石叶 blade
GoJh14：1556
65 mm × 32 mm × 11 mm

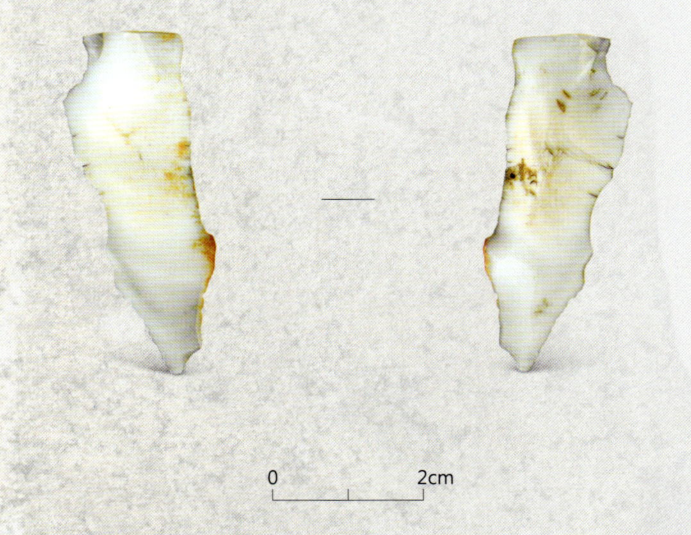

石叶 blade
GoJh14：1559
47 mm × 17 mm × 6 mm

0 1cm

石叶
blade

GoJh14：2260
53 mm × 26 mm × 9 mm

石叶
blade

GoJh14：1444
68 mm × 32 mm × 10 mm

石叶 GoJh14：2275
blade 46 mm × 21 mm × 5 mm

石叶 GoJh14：1543
blade 86 mm × 38 mm × 15 mm

SCRAPER

刮削器

刮削器 scraper
GoJh14：11
26 mm × 22 mm × 8 mm

刮削器 scraper
GoJh14：92
52 mm × 35 mm × 7 mm

0 2cm

刮削器 scraper \ GoJh14 ： 150
76 mm × 18 mm × 11 mm

0 1cm

刮削器 scraper \ GoJh14 ： 152
11 mm × 14 mm × 4 mm

0 1cm

刮削器 scraper \ GoJh14 ： 153
24 mm × 17 mm × 6 mm

刮削器
scraper
GoJh14 ： 1013
44 mm × 25 mm × 19 mm

刮削器
scraper
GoJh14 ： 1027
51 mm × 52 mm × 19 mm

刮削器
scraper
GoJh14 ： 1047
18 mm × 15 mm × 4 mm

刮削器
scraper
GoJh14 ： 1035
54 mm × 37 mm × 19 mm

0 1cm

刮削器 GoJh14：1048
scraper 26 mm × 18 mm × 5 mm

0 1cm

刮削器 GoJh14：1080
scraper 11 mm × 9 mm × 3 mm

刮削器 scraper ╲ GoJh14：1075
16 mm × 5 mm × 4 mm

刮削器 scraper ╲ GoJh14：1051
45 mm × 35 mm × 10 mm

刮削器 scraper ╲ GoJh14：1089
20 mm × 14 mm × 4 mm

0 2cm

刮削器 scraper

GoJh14：1405
44 mm × 43 mm × 12 mm

0 1cm

刮削器 scraper

GoJh14：1458
22 mm × 19 mm × 8 mm

刮削器
scraper

GoJh14 ∶ 1466
46 mm × 24 mm × 8 mm

刮削器
scraper

GoJh14 ∶ 1478
61 mm × 37 mm × 14 mm

刮削器 scraper　GoJh14：1529
13 mm × 16 mm × 4 mm

刮削器 scraper　GoJh14：1587
19 mm × 16 mm × 5 mm

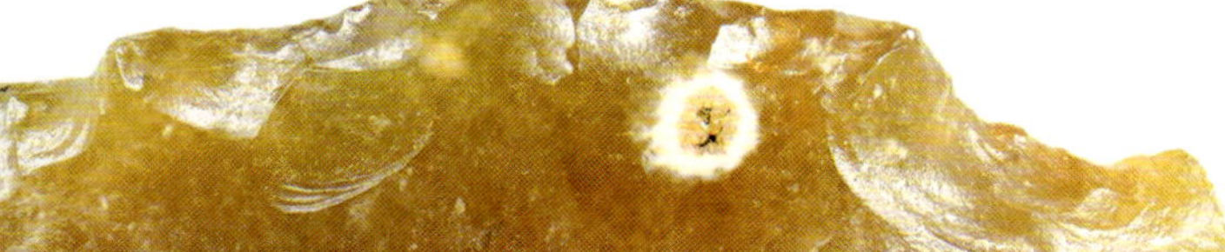

刮削器 scraper　GoJh14：1565
63 mm × 36 mm × 14 mm

刮削器 scraper　GoJh14：1807
22 mm × 16 mm × 6 mm

刮削器 scraper
GoJh14 ： 1808
43 mm × 33 mm × 12 mm

0 2cm

刮削器 scraper
GoJh14 ： 1821
44 mm × 49 mm × 14 mm

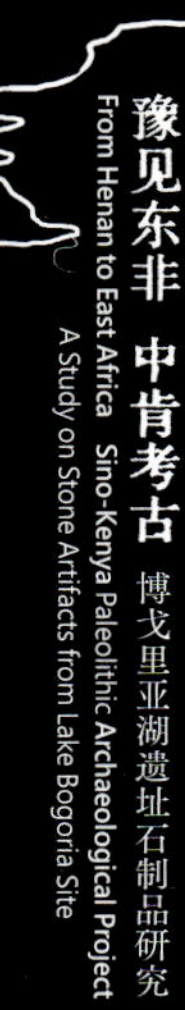

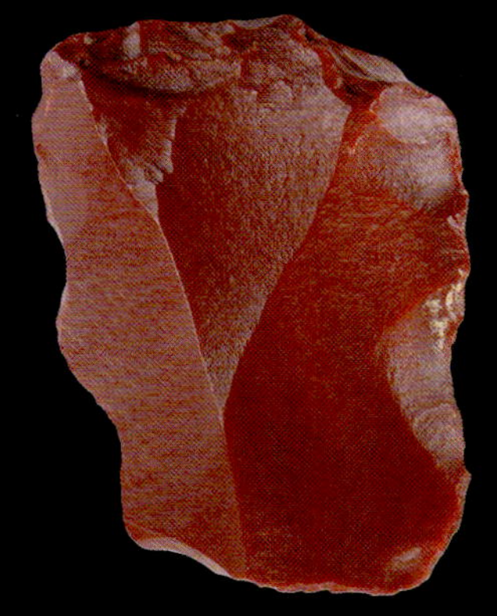

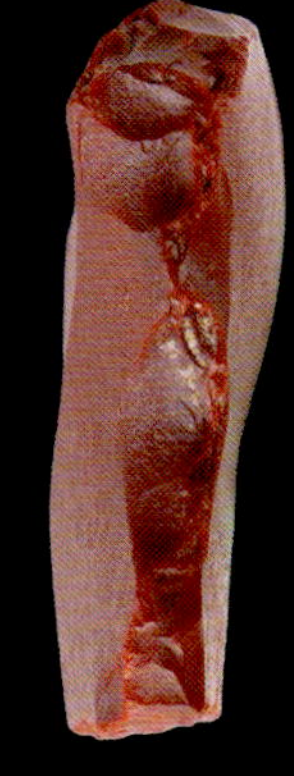

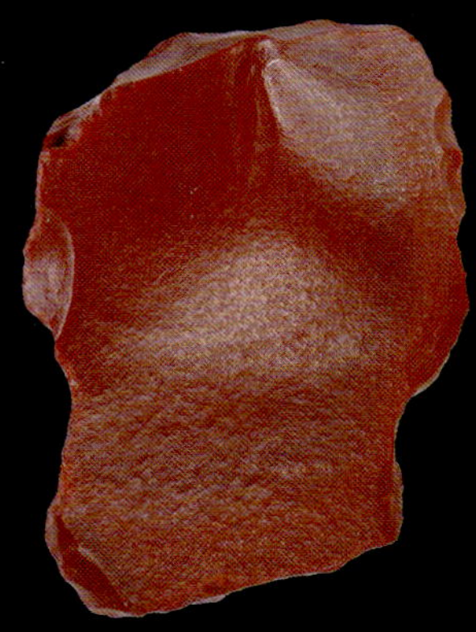

0 1cm

刮削器 scraper ╲ GoJh14：1935
17 mm × 14 mm × 5 mm

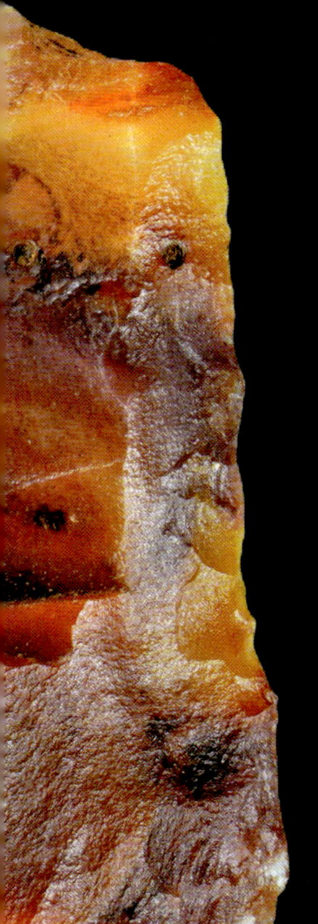

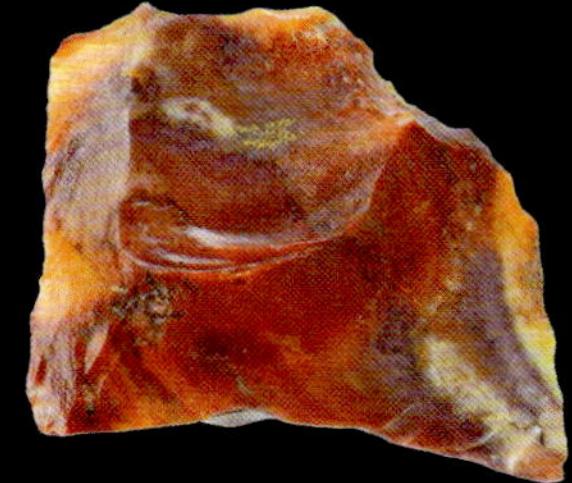

0 1cm

刮削器 scraper ╲ GoJh14：1955
19 mm × 17 mm × 4 mm

0 2cm

刮削器 scraper
GoJh14：1979
78 mm × 79 mm × 34 mm

刮削器
scraper

GoJh14：1994
23 mm × 15 mm × 9 mm

刮削器
scraper

GoJh14：2211
54 mm × 34 mm × 8 mm

0 1cm

刮削器 scraper

GoJh14：2274
16 mm × 14 mm × 5 mm

0 1cm

刮削器 scraper

GoJh14：2484
23 mm × 13 mm × 7 mm

NOTCH

凹缺器

凹缺器 notch
GoJh14：19
18 mm × 13 mm × 3 mm

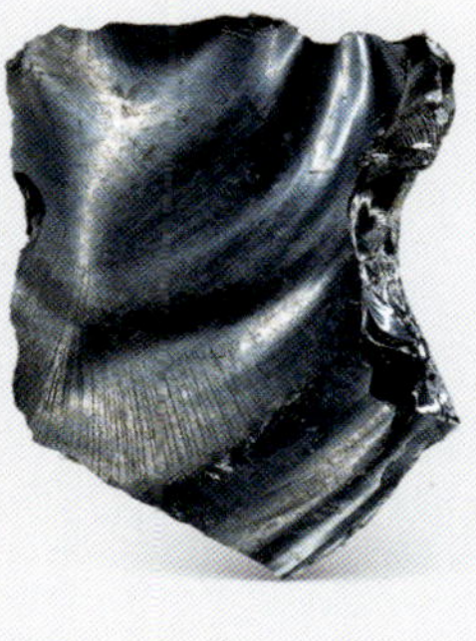

凹缺器 notch
GoJh14：158
19 mm × 15 mm × 3 mm

0 1cm

凹缺器
notch

GoJh14：178
25 mm × 23 mm × 6 mm

凹缺器 notch
GoJh14 ： 1574
30 mm × 20 mm × 5 mm

凹缺器 notch
GoJh14 ： 1950
19 mm × 10 mm × 3 mm

POINT

尖状器

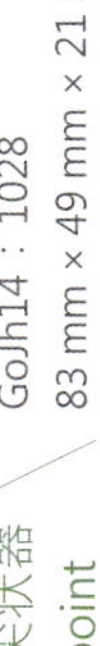

尖状器 / point
GoJh14：1028
83 mm × 49 mm × 21 mm

2cm
0

0 1cm

尖状器
point

GoJh14：1086
31 mm × 26 mm × 9 mm

0 2cm

尖状器 point ╲ GoJh14：1491
50 mm × 60 mm × 17 mm

尖状器 point ╲ GoJh14：1504
12 mm × 15 mm × 4 mm

0 1cm

尖状器 point ╲ GoJh14：1553
27 mm × 27 mm × 8 mm

LEVALLOIS POINT

——

勒瓦娄哇尖状器

0 2cm

勒瓦娄哇尖状器
Levallois point

GoJh14：9
55 mm × 42 mm × 10 mm

0 2cm

勒瓦娄哇尖状器
Levallois point

GoJh14：403
66 mm × 45 mm × 14 mm

0 1cm

勒瓦娄哇尖状器 Levallois point

GoJh14：1053
33 mm × 26 mm × 10 mm

0 1cm

勒瓦娄哇尖状器 Levallois point

GoJh14：1092
58 mm × 41 mm × 12 mm

勒瓦娄哇尖状器
Levallois point

GoJh14：1856
75 mm × 56 mm × 17 mm

1cm

0

勒瓦娄哇尖状器
Levallois point

GoJh14：1871
63 mm × 42 mm × 15 mm

0 1cm

勒瓦娄哇尖状器 GoJh14：1877
Levallois point 71 mm × 56 mm × 15 mm

勒瓦娄哇尖状器
Levallois point

GoJh14：2296
83 mm × 53 mm × 15 mm

2cm
0

勒瓦娄哇尖状器 / GoJh14：2390
Levallois point / 89 mm × 28 mm × 9 mm

0 2cm

勒瓦娄哇尖状器
Levallois point

GoJh14：1901
71 mm × 54 mm × 11 mm

0 2cm

勒瓦娄哇尖状器
Levallois point

GoJh14 ： 2261
51 mm × 29 mm × 9 mm

0 2cm

勒瓦娄哇尖状器
Levallois point

GoJh14 ： 2515
56 mm × 43 mm × 14 mm

CHOPPER

砍砸器

0 2cm

砍砸器 chopper

GoJh14：1986
80 mm × 90 mm × 47 mm

砍砸器 chopper

GoJh14：1044
78 mm × 65 mm × 30 mm

砍砸器 chopper

GoJh14：1987
75 mm × 93 mm × 41 mm

砍砸器 chopper ╲ GoJh14 ： 1067
93 mm × 75 mm × 42 mm

OTHER STONE ARTIFACTS

其他

石叶石核
blade core

GoJh14：747
58 mm × 61 mm × 19 mm

勒瓦娄哇石叶
Levallois blade

GoJh14：1843
72 mm × 36 mm × 15 mm

0 1cm

小石叶 \ GoJh14：1056
bladelet \ 18 mm × 9 mm × 2 mm

0 1cm

钻器 \ GoJh14：1528
borer \ 24 mm × 22 mm × 5 mm

0 1cm

钻器 borer

GoJh14：2270
15 mm × 19 mm × 4 mm

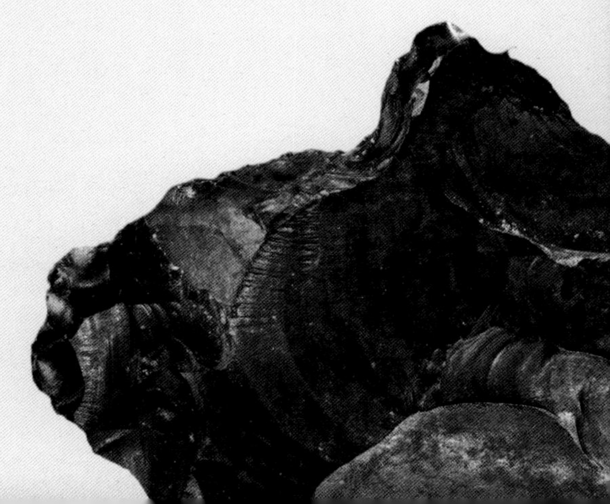

The members of the Chinese team spend 1–2 months each year working in the field in Kenya. During this time, they conduct archaeological surveys, excavations, and preliminary studies on unearthed archaeological materials in order to identify new Paleolithic sites for future research. Because lithic artifacts are densely distributed on the surface around the Lake Bogoria site, the archaeological team always carries a high-precision GPS (GPS accuracy of within 1 m) to mark the location of artifacts and record the investigation path. After taking photos and recording the coordinates of lithic artifacts, most of them were left in situ. With the consent of the Kenyan side, only a few typical specimens were collected, numbered, photographed, and statistically analyzed before handed over to National Museums of Kenya.

In 2019, researchers discovered 14 Paleolithic sites around Lake Bogoria, four of which seemed to be small lithic production workshops based on initial analysis. They uncovered approximately 1,500 pieces of lithic artifacts (excluding fragments and debris), of which only 60 were selected for further study. The raw materials for the lithics included andesite, basalt, trachyte, flint, obsidian, and more. The findings included cores, flakes (mostly intact), Levallois points, scrapers, hand axes, and small backed knives.

The survey of 2023 covered an area of approximately 10 square kilometers, leading to the discovery of 22 Paleolithic sites. Over 2,000 lithic artifacts (excluding fragments and debris) were found, with only 99 collected for further analysis. Three of the Paleolithic sites appear to be small lithic production workshops, characterized by a high density of lithic artifacts on the surface, primarily consisting of flakes and cores. Additionally, a few tools, such as scrapers and flakes, were identified. The most notable discoveries include cores, flakes, and typical products of Levallois technology. Furthermore, typical blades, blade cores, and microliths were also found.

ARCHAEOLOGICAL SURVEYS

肆

调查石制品

中方队员每年在肯尼亚野外工作时间为 1—2 个月，在肯期间除了考古发掘和整理材料，也需要同步展开野外调查，为后续考古发掘工作储备新的旧石器地点。由于博戈里亚湖遗址地表石制品分布较为密集，因此在调查时，考古队员需随身携带高精度 GPS（单机精度可达 1 米内），记录调查路径并标记地表石制品位置。按照肯方要求，对调查发现的石制品进行拍照并记录坐标位置后，石制品多留在原地。经肯方负责人同意后，我们仅对特别典型的石器标本进行采集，编号、拍照和统计分析工作完成之后移交给肯方保管。

2019 年，在博戈里亚湖遗址共发现旧石器地点 14 处，其中 4 处为小型石器制作场，发现石器的数量粗略估计约 1500 件（不含断块、碎屑），仅采集 60 件。石制品原料为安山岩、粗面岩、玄武岩、燧石和黑曜岩等，类型为石核、石片（多数为完整石片）、勒瓦娄哇尖状器、刮削器、手斧和琢背小刀等。

2023 年，调查面积约 10 平方千米，共标记旧石器地点 22 个，发现石器的数量初步统计达 2000 件（不含断块、碎屑），仅采集 99 件。其中有 3 处为小型石器制作场，地表密集分布着大量石制品，绝大多数为石片、石核，少量为刮削器、砍砸器等，其中以典型的旧石器时代中期勒瓦娄哇技术产生的石核、石片、石器等最为突出，也有典型的石叶、石叶石核及细石器。

BLADE CORE

—

石叶石核

0 2cm

石叶石核 / blade core

GoJh14：303
49 mm × 48 mm × 44 mm

石叶石核
blade core

GoJh14 ： 243
48 mm × 55 mm × 73 mm

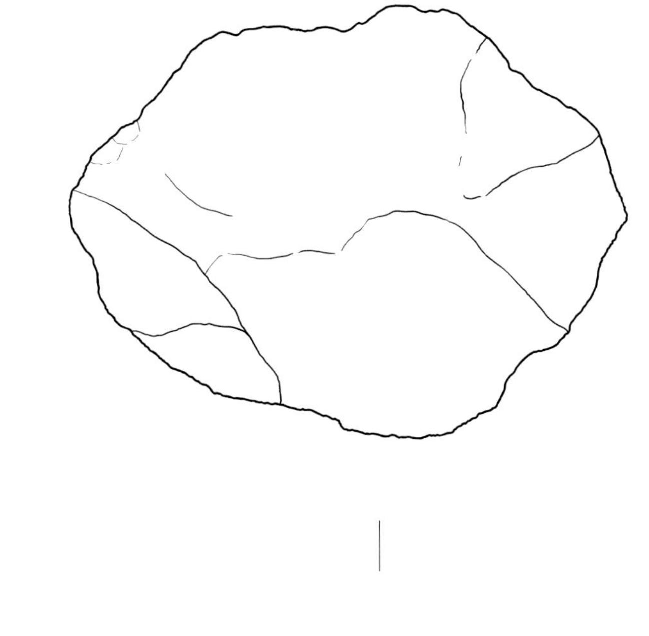

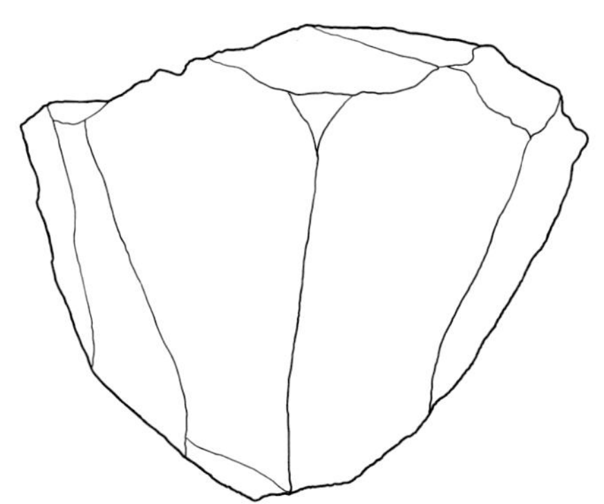

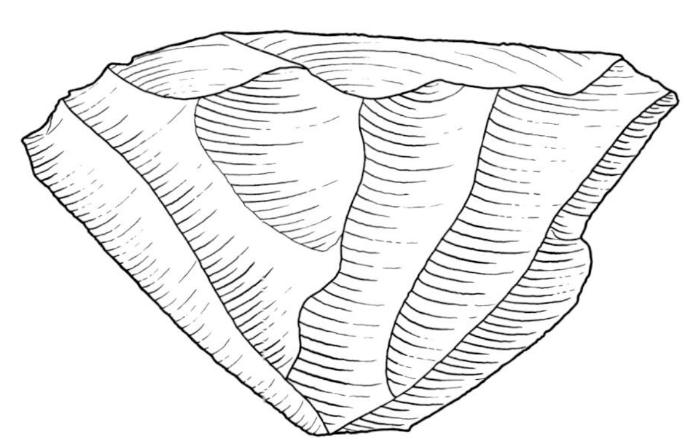

石叶石核 blade core

GoJh14：213
65 mm × 68 mm × 54 mm

LEVALLOIS CORE

勒瓦娄哇石核

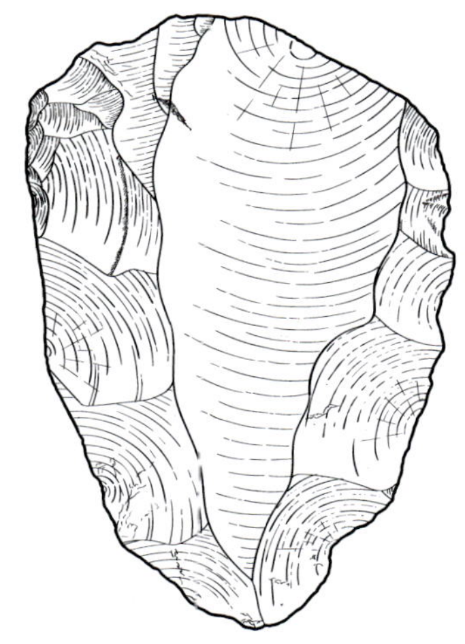

0 2cm

勒瓦娄哇石核
Levallois core

GoJh14：248
62 mm × 42 mm × 23 mm

勒瓦娄哇石核
Levallois core

GoJh14：249
57 mm × 48 mm × 33 mm

0 2cm

勒瓦娄哇石核 GoJh14：232
Levallois core 70 mm × 91 mm × 35 mm

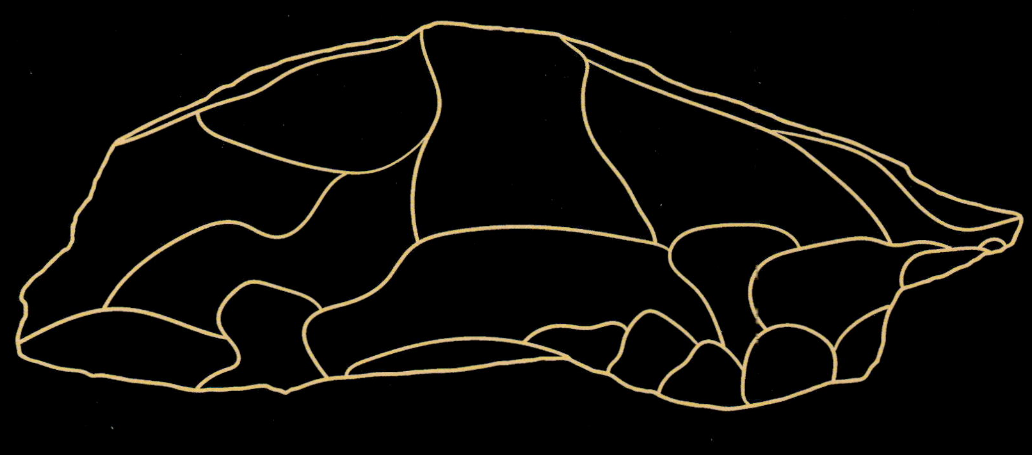

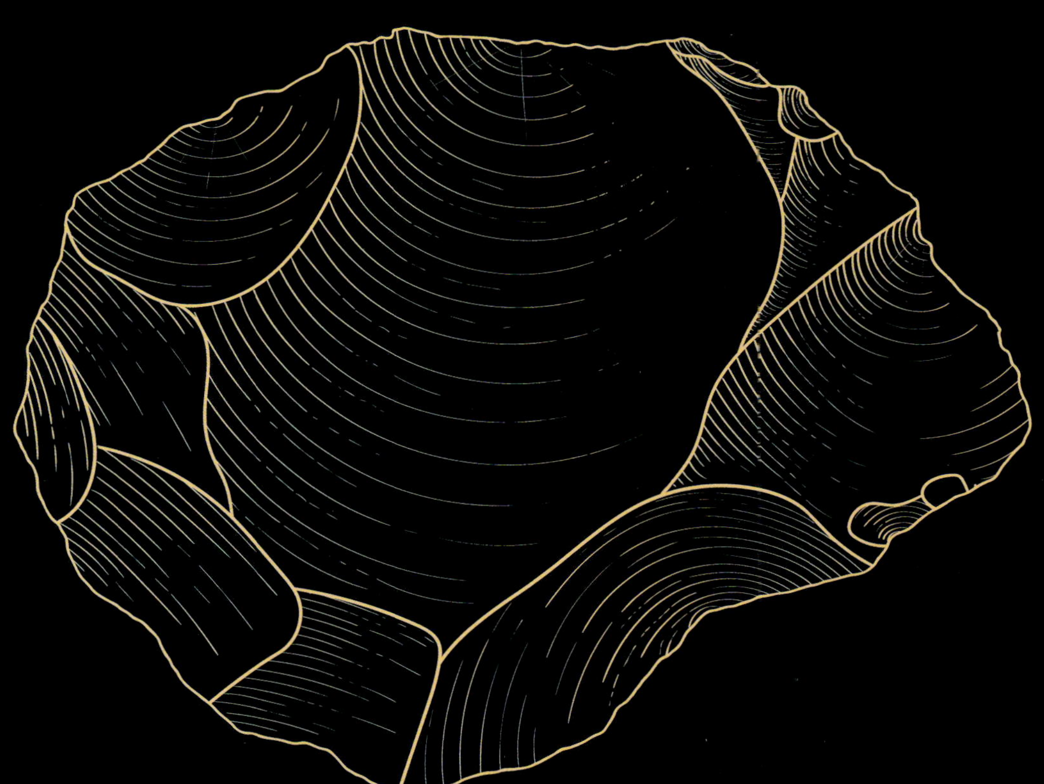

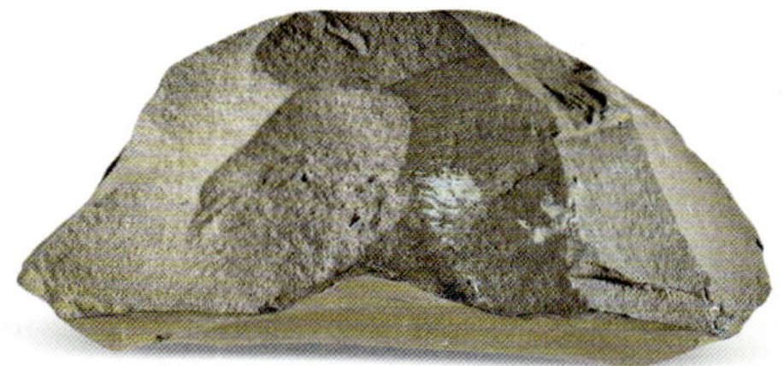

0 2cm

勒瓦娄哇石核
Levallois core

GoJh14：242
77 mm × 57 mm × 27 mm

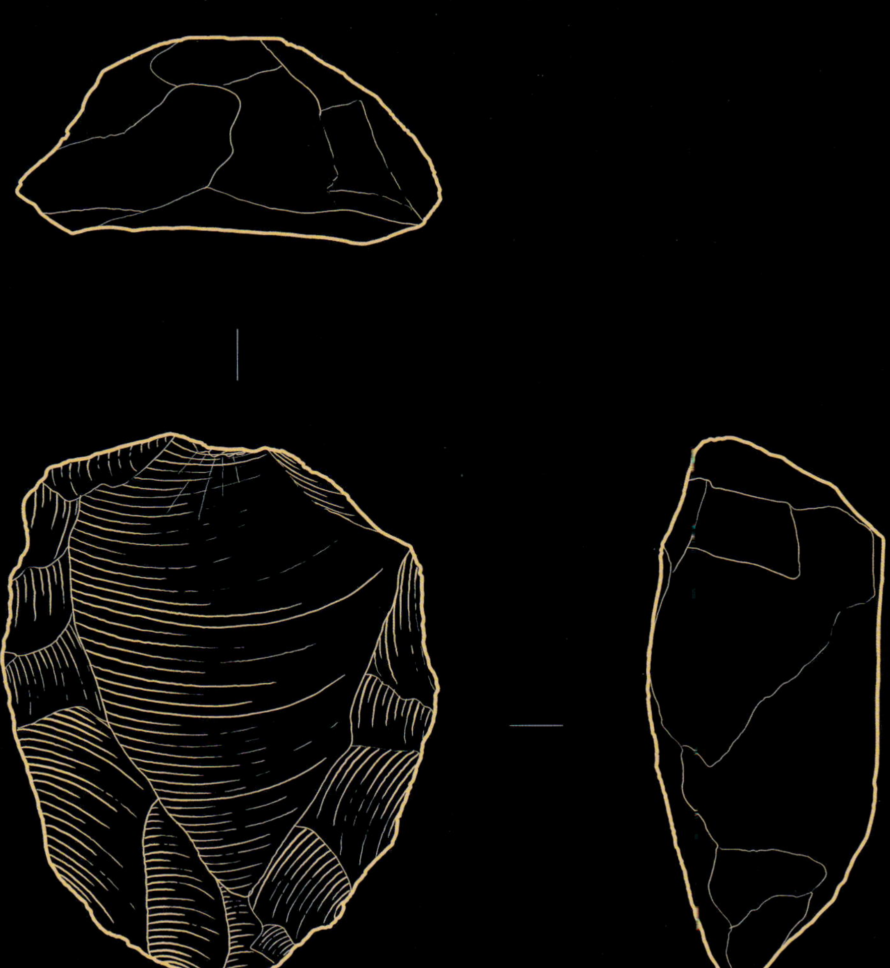

勒瓦娄哇石核
Levallois core

GoJh14：254
68 mm × 49 mm × 34 mm

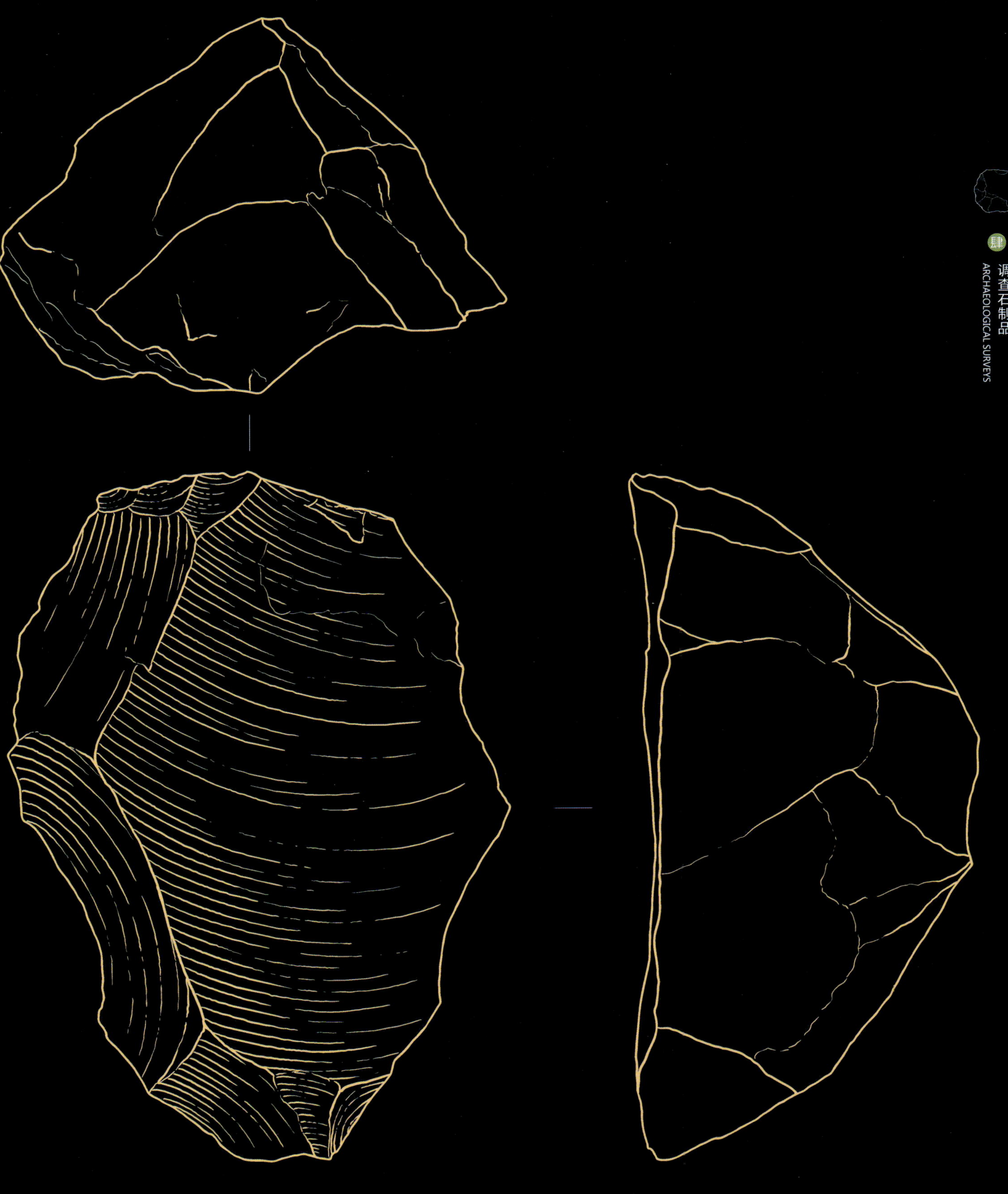

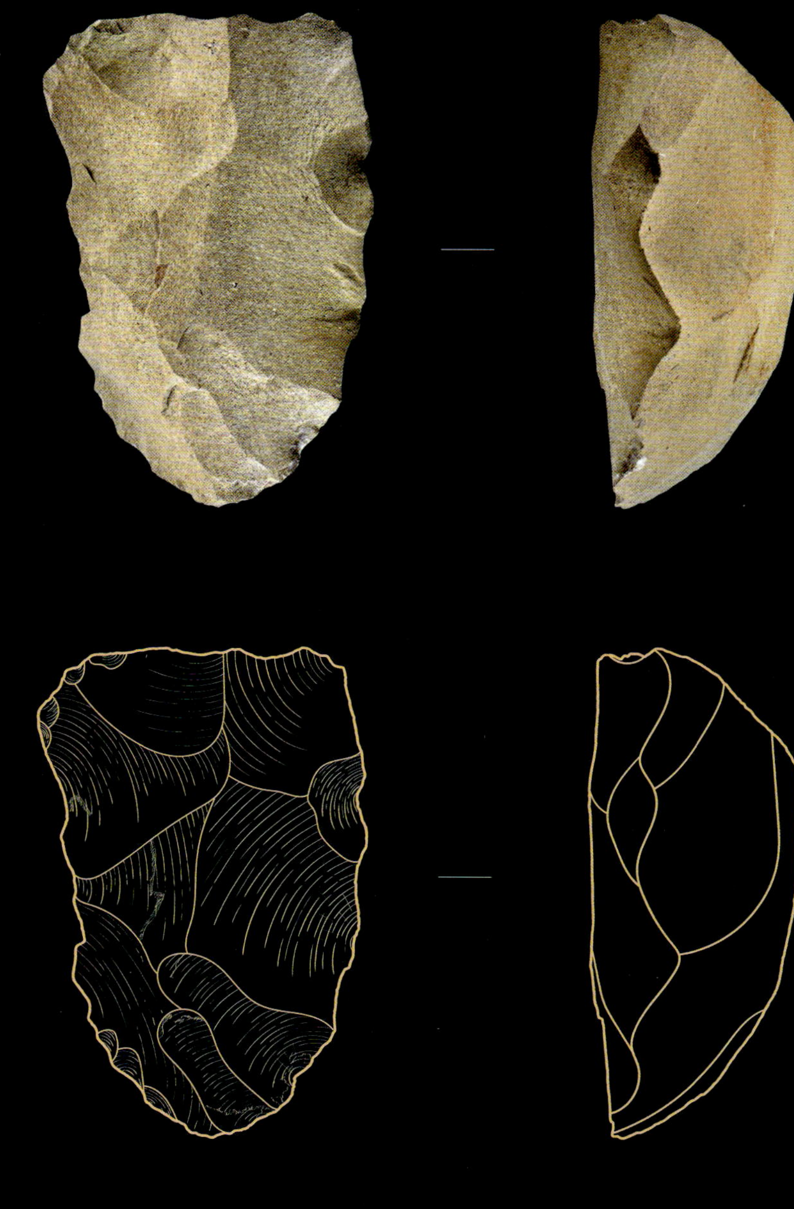

0 2cm

勒瓦娄哇石核 \ GoJh14：255
Levallois core \ 68 mm × 43 mm × 28 mm

勒瓦娄哇石核 GoJh14：257
Levallois core 67 mm × 57 mm × 29 mm

0 2cm

勒瓦娄哇石核
Levallois core

GoJh14：259
56 mm × 53 mm × 25 mm

0 2cm

勒瓦娄哇石核
Levallois core

GoJh14 ： 266
70 mm × 55 mm × 42 mm

0 2cm

勒瓦娄哇石核 GoJh14：297
Levallois core 79 mm × 73 mm × 35 mm

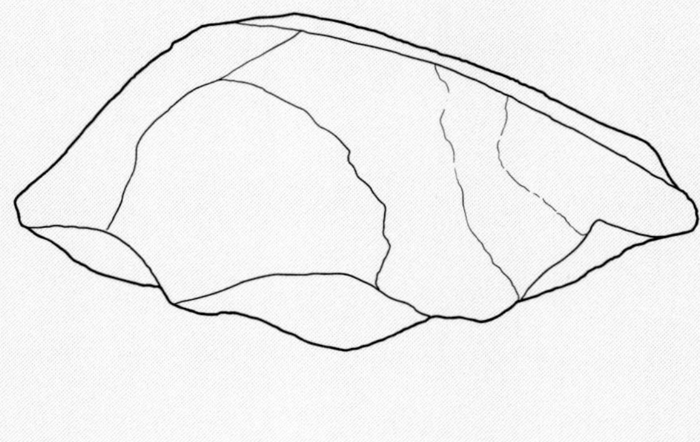

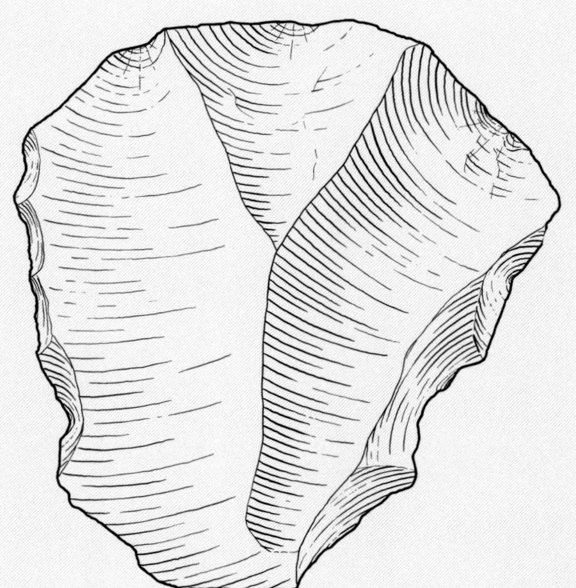

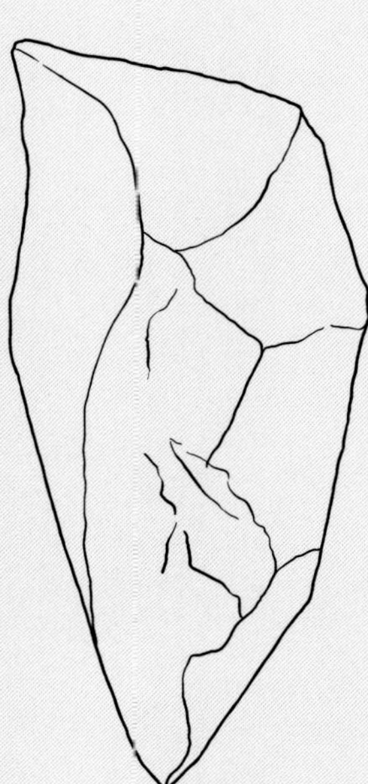

0 2cm

勒瓦娄哇石核
Levallois core

GoJh14 ： 267
74 mm × 45 mm × 29 mm

0 2cm

勒瓦娄哇石核
Levallois core

GoJh14：288
109 mm × 71 mm × 30 mm

0 1cm

勒瓦娄哇石核
Levallois core

GoJh14：292
59 mm × 44 mm × 21 mm

勒瓦娄哇石核
Levallois core

GoJh14：330
146 mm × 65 mm × 66 mm

FLAKE

石片

0 2cm

石片 \ GoJh14：186
flake \ 33 mm × 37 mm × 11 mm

0 1cm

石片 \ GoJh14：319
flake \ 24 mm × 19 mm × 9 mm

0 1cm

石片 flake | GoJh14：325
41 mm × 23 mm × 10 mm

石片 flake
GoJh14 ： 338
22 mm × 25 mm × 6 mm

LEVALLOIS FLAKE

勒瓦娄哇石片

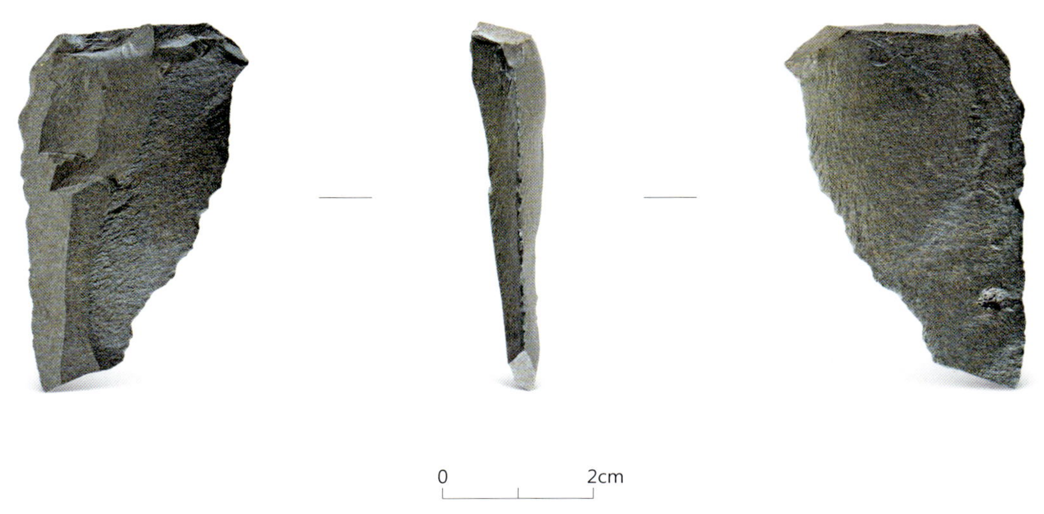

勒瓦娄哇石片
Levallois flake

GoJh14：182
51 mm × 32 mm × 11 mm

勒瓦娄哇石片
Levallois flake

GoJh14：185
63 mm × 40 mm × 19 mm

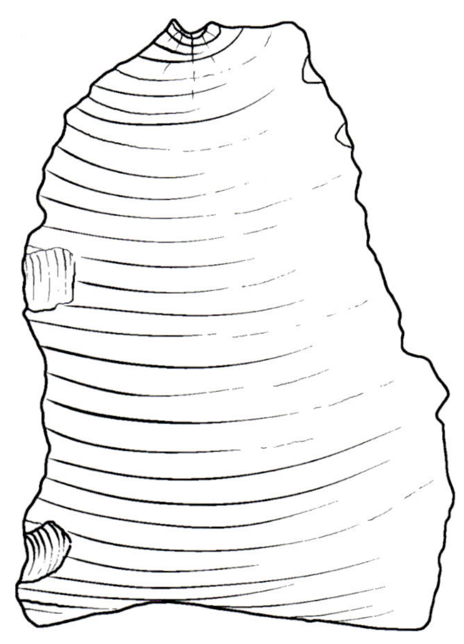

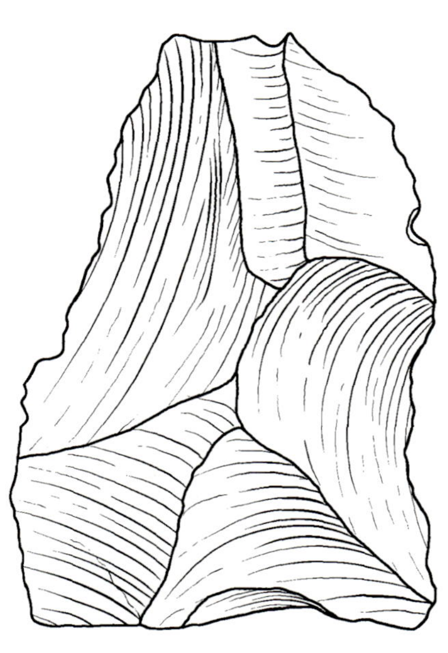

0 1cm

勒瓦娄哇石片
Levallois flake

GoJh14：187
39 mm × 27 mm × 5 mm

勒瓦娄哇石片 GoJh14 : 203
Levallois flake 54 mm × 43 mm × 17 mm

勒瓦娄哇石片 GoJh14 : 204
Levallois flake 49 mm × 37 mm × 10 mm

勒瓦娄哇石片
Levallois flake

GoJh14：272
100 mm × 64 mm × 32 mm

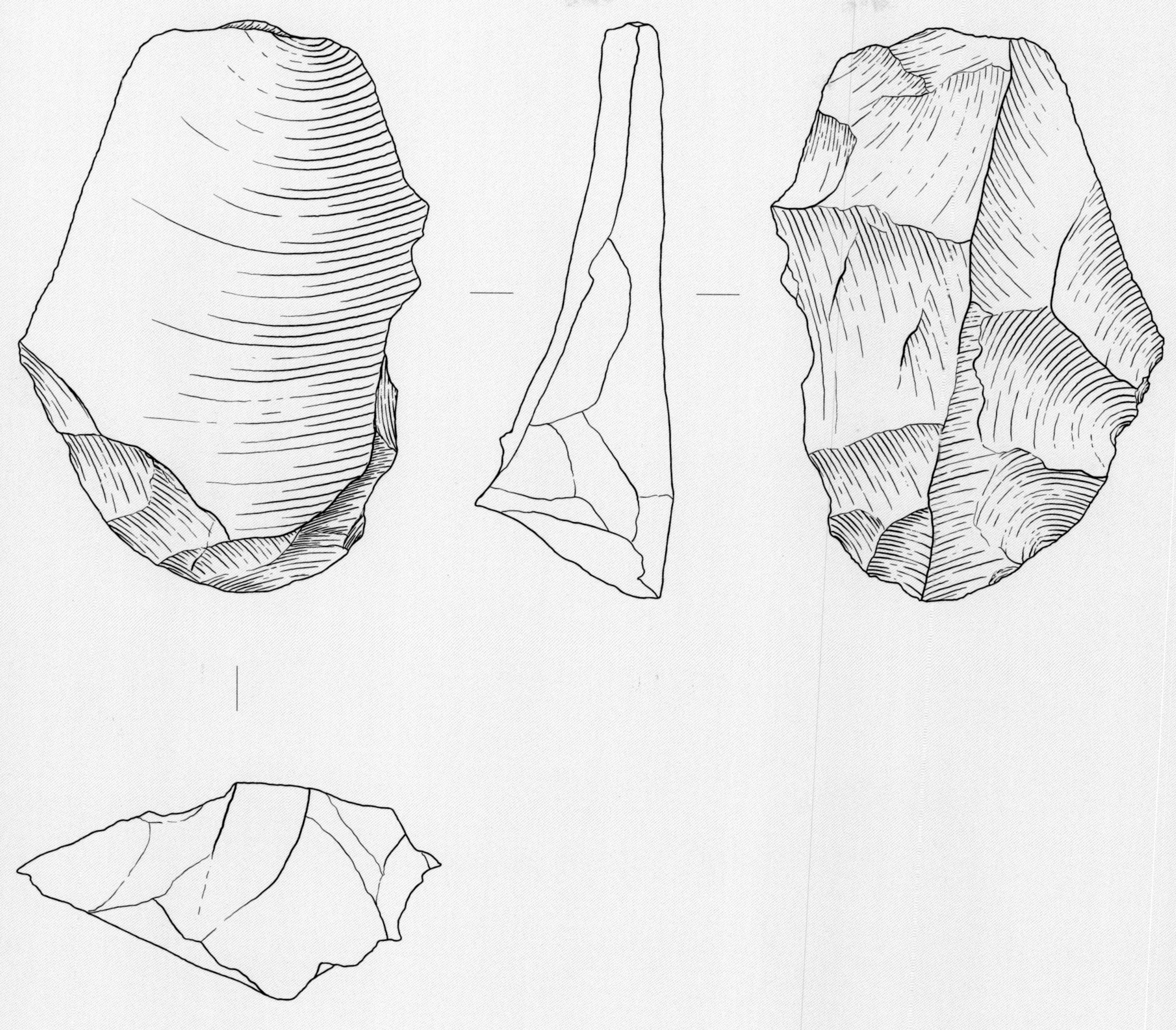

勒瓦娄哇石片
Levallois flake

GoJh14 ：244
53 mm × 38 mm × 10 mm

0 2cm

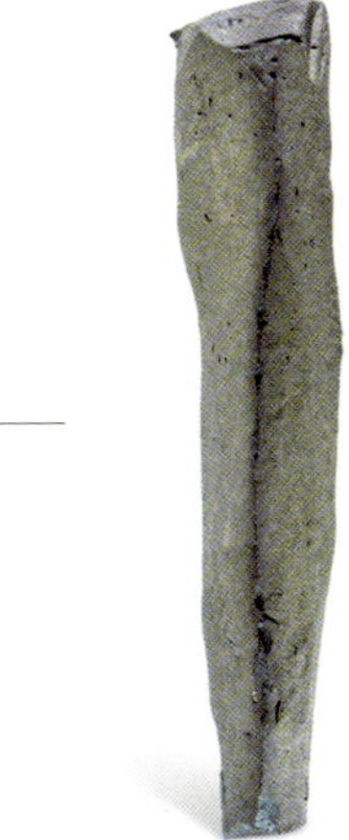

0 2cm

勒瓦娄哇石片
Levallois flake

GoJh14 ：274
60 mm × 39 mm × 11 mm

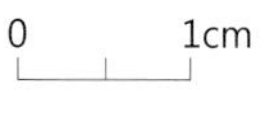

0 1cm

勒瓦娄哇石片 Levallois flake ╲ GoJh14：276 84 mm × 50 mm × 13 mm

勒瓦娄哇石片 GoJh14：283
Levallois flake 66 mm × 49 mm × 12 mm

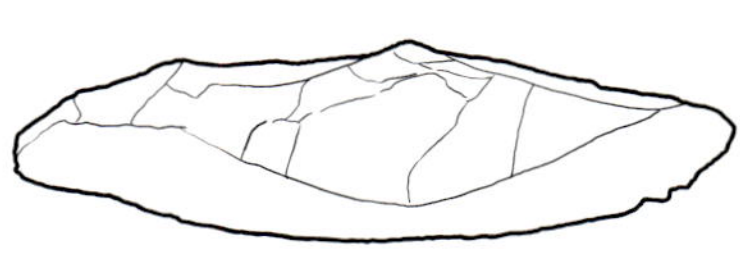
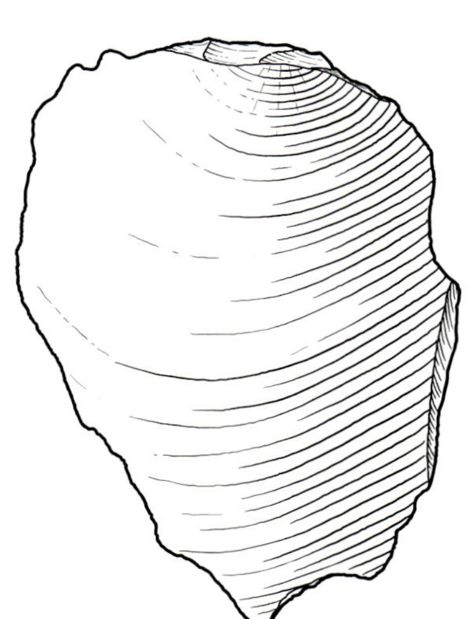
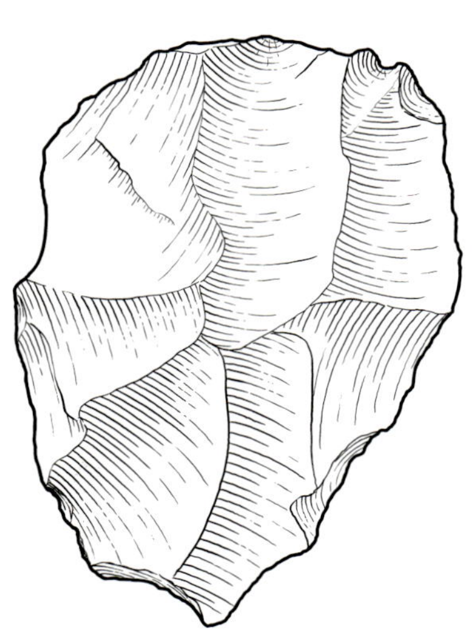

0 2cm

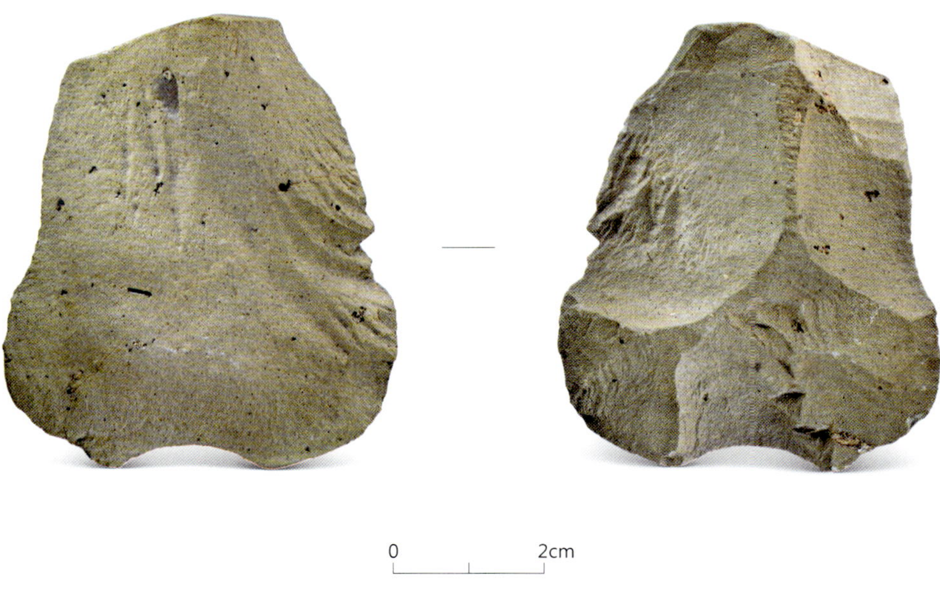

勒瓦娄哇石片
Levallois flake

GoJh14：316
62 mm × 52 mm × 16 mm

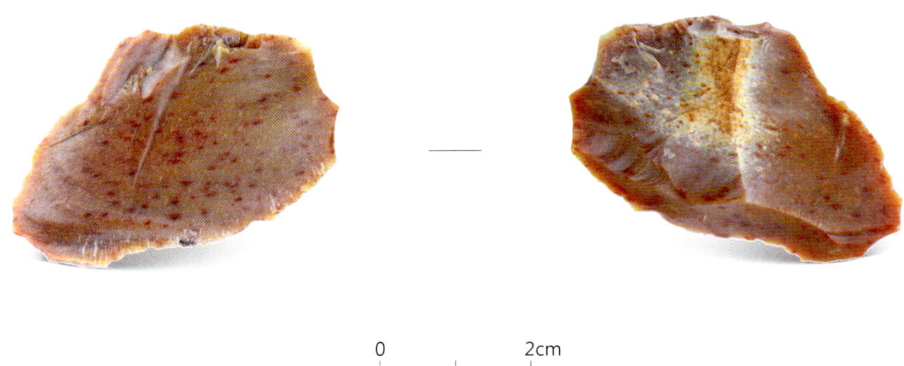

勒瓦娄哇石片
Levallois flake

GoJh14：337
31 mm × 45 mm × 9 mm

BLADE

石叶

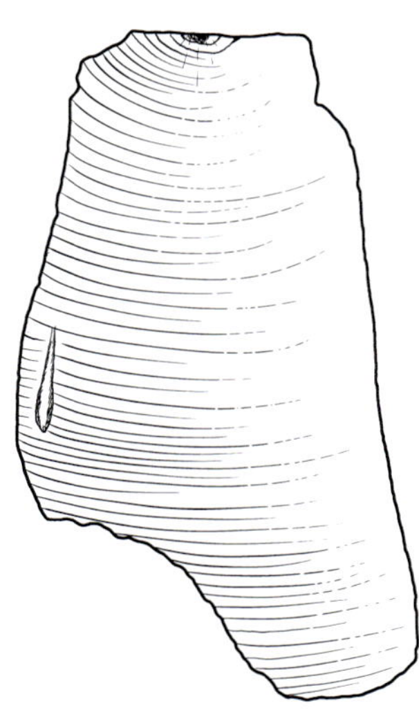

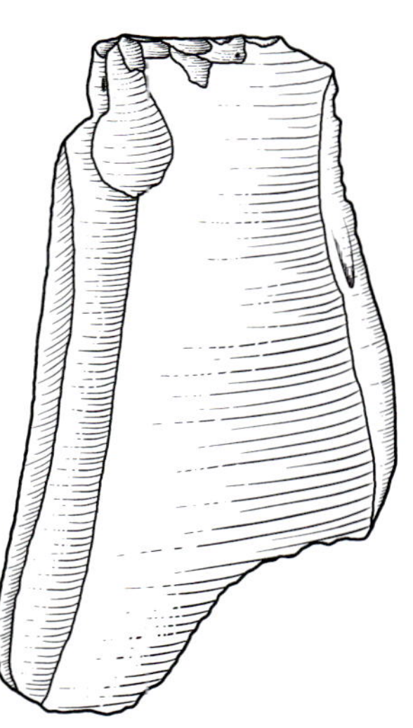

0 2cm

石叶 blade

GoJh14：183
67 mm × 33 mm × 8 mm

0 2cm

石叶 GoJh14：211
blade 79 mm × 22 mm × 11 mm

0 2cm

石叶 GoJh14：287
blade 35 mm × 17 mm × 4 mm

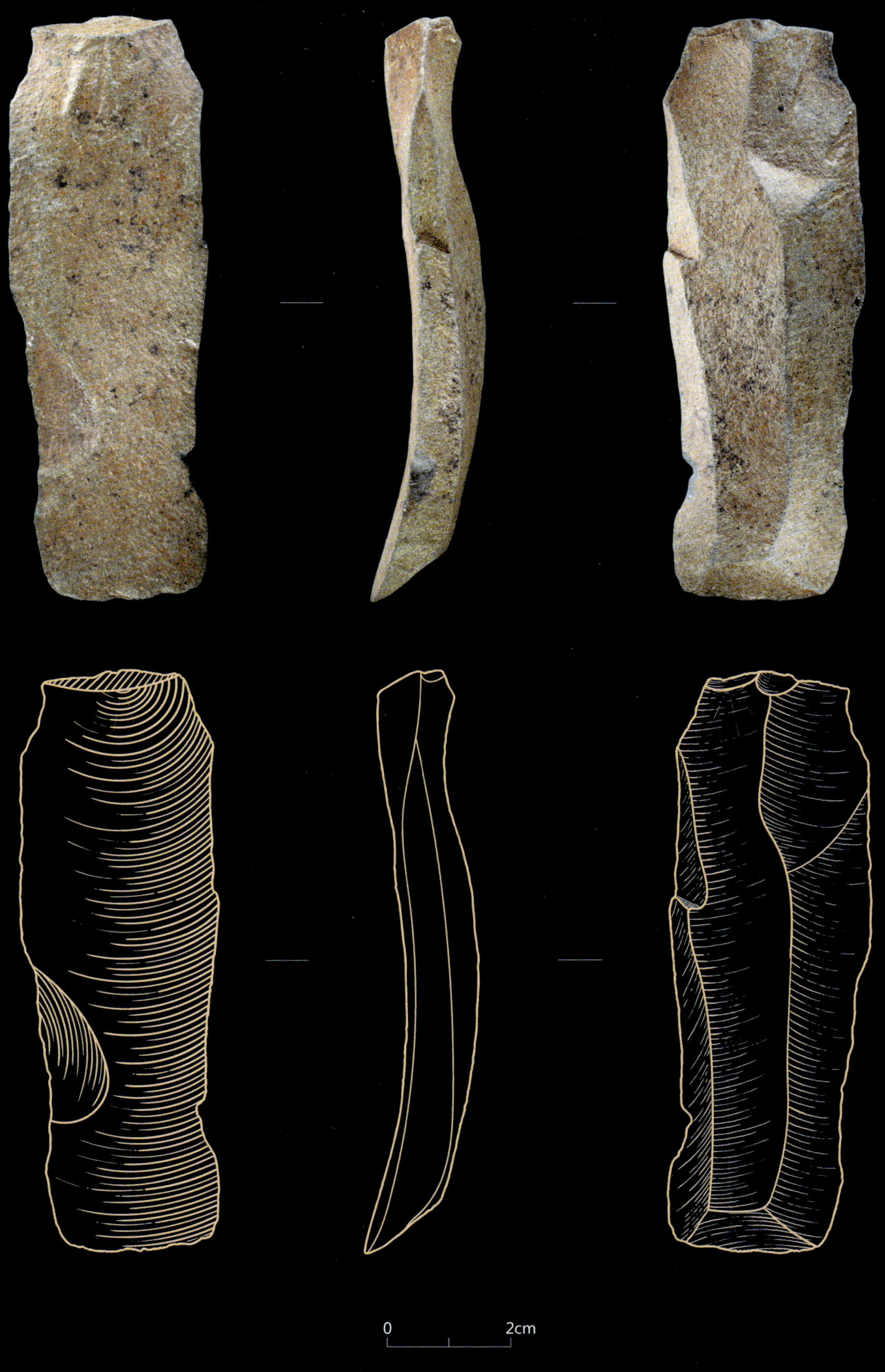

石叶 GoJh14：217
blade 98 mm × 33 mm × 13 mm

石叶
blade

GoJh14 ：246
120 mm × 44 mm × 14 mm

0 2cm

石叶 GoJh14：311
blade 82 mm × 19 mm × 7 mm

0 2cm

石叶 ╲ GoJh14：310
blade ╲ 72 mm × 24 mm × 8 mm

0 2cm

石叶 blade
GoJh14：312
93 mm × 31 mm × 5 mm

0 2cm

石叶 blade
GoJh14：317
80 mm × 35 mm × 12 mm

0 2cm

石叶 GoJh14 ： 208
blade 54 mm × 23 mm × 10 mm

0 2cm

石叶 GoJh14 ： 209
blade 49 mm × 17 mm × 5 mm

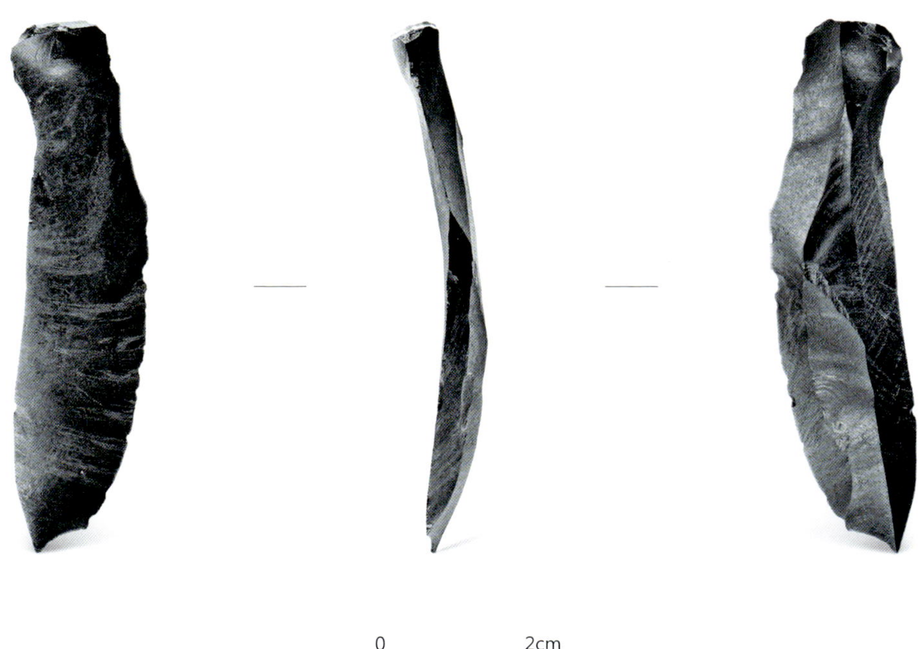

石叶 GoJh14 ： 233
blade 73 mm × 17 mm × 7 mm

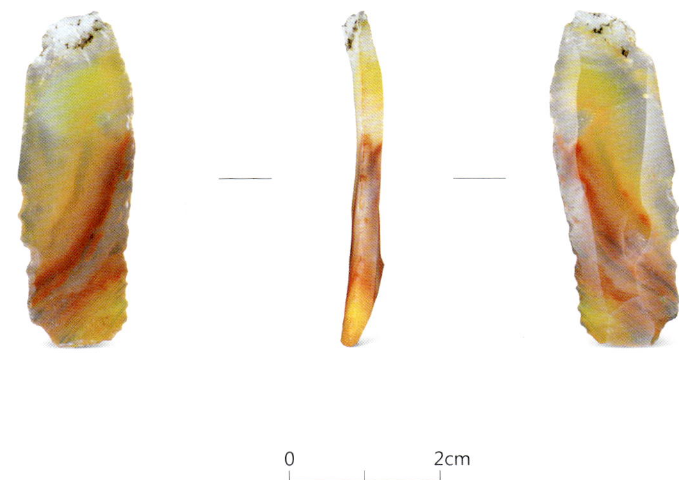

石叶 GoJh14 ： 336
blade 46 mm × 16 mm × 6 mm

LEVALLOIS BLADE

勒瓦娄哇石叶

勒瓦娄哇石叶
Levallois blade

GoJh14：207
108 mm × 47 mm × 16 mm

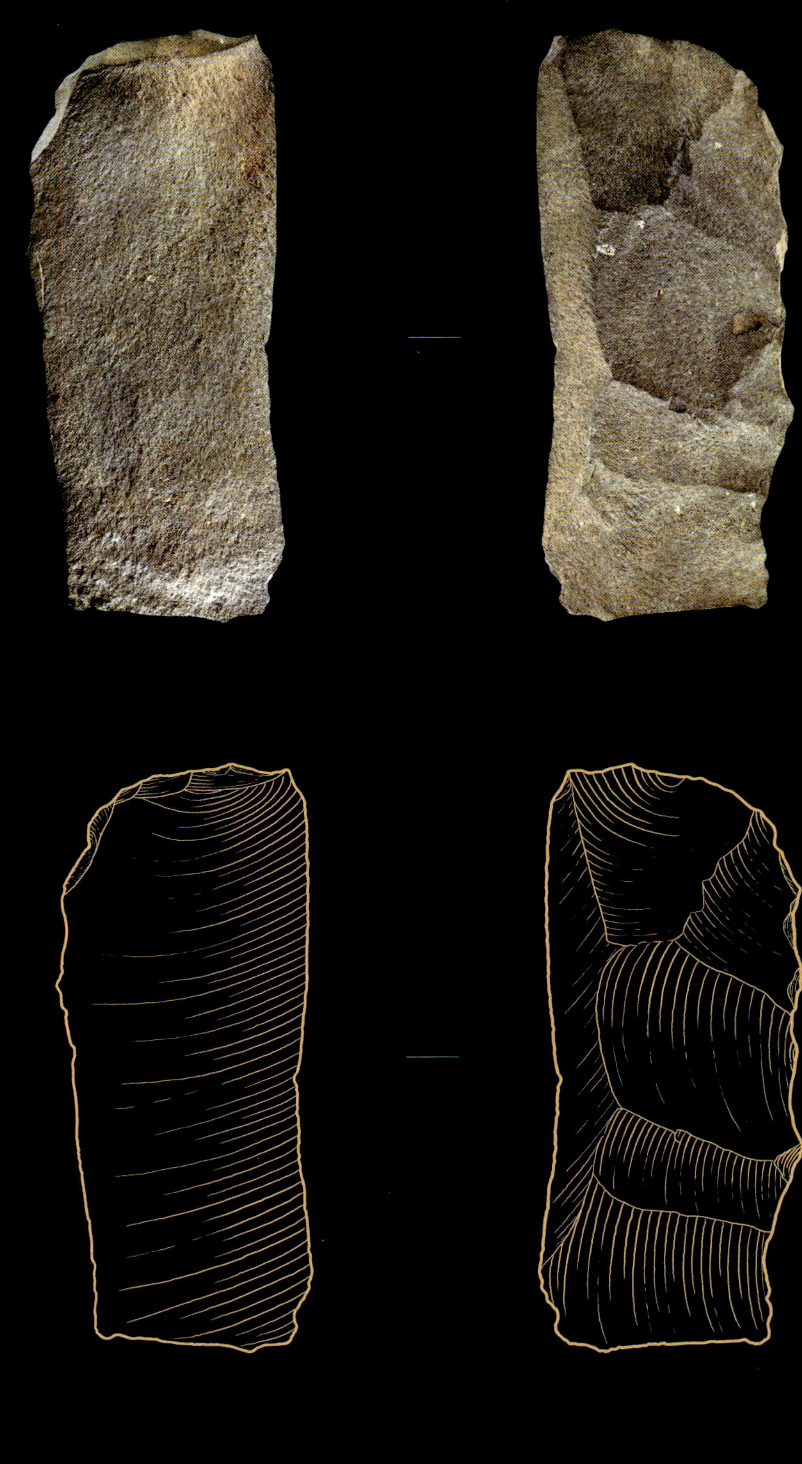

0 2cm

勒瓦娄哇石叶 ╲ GoJh14：245
Levallois blade ╲ 81 mm × 35 mm × 15 mm

勒瓦娄哇石叶
Levallois blade

GoJh14：247
80 mm × 39 mm × 15 mm

勒瓦娄哇石叶
Levallois blade

GoJh14：279
47 mm × 23 mm × 7 mm

勒瓦娄哇石叶
Levallois blade

GoJh14：275
77 mm × 38 mm × 16 mm

0 2cm

勒瓦娄哇石叶
Levallois blade

GoJh14 ： 277
79 mm × 51 mm × 14 mm

勒瓦娄哇石叶 GoJh14 ： 280
Levallois blade 68 mm × 28 mm × 9 mm

勒瓦娄哇石叶 GoJh14 ： 281
Levallois blade 70 mm × 26 mm × 8 mm

勒瓦娄哇石叶
Levallois blade

GoJh14 ：282
70 mm × 35 mm × 11 mm

0 2cm

勒瓦娄哇石叶
Levallois blade

GoJh14：284
70 mm × 25 mm × 14 mm

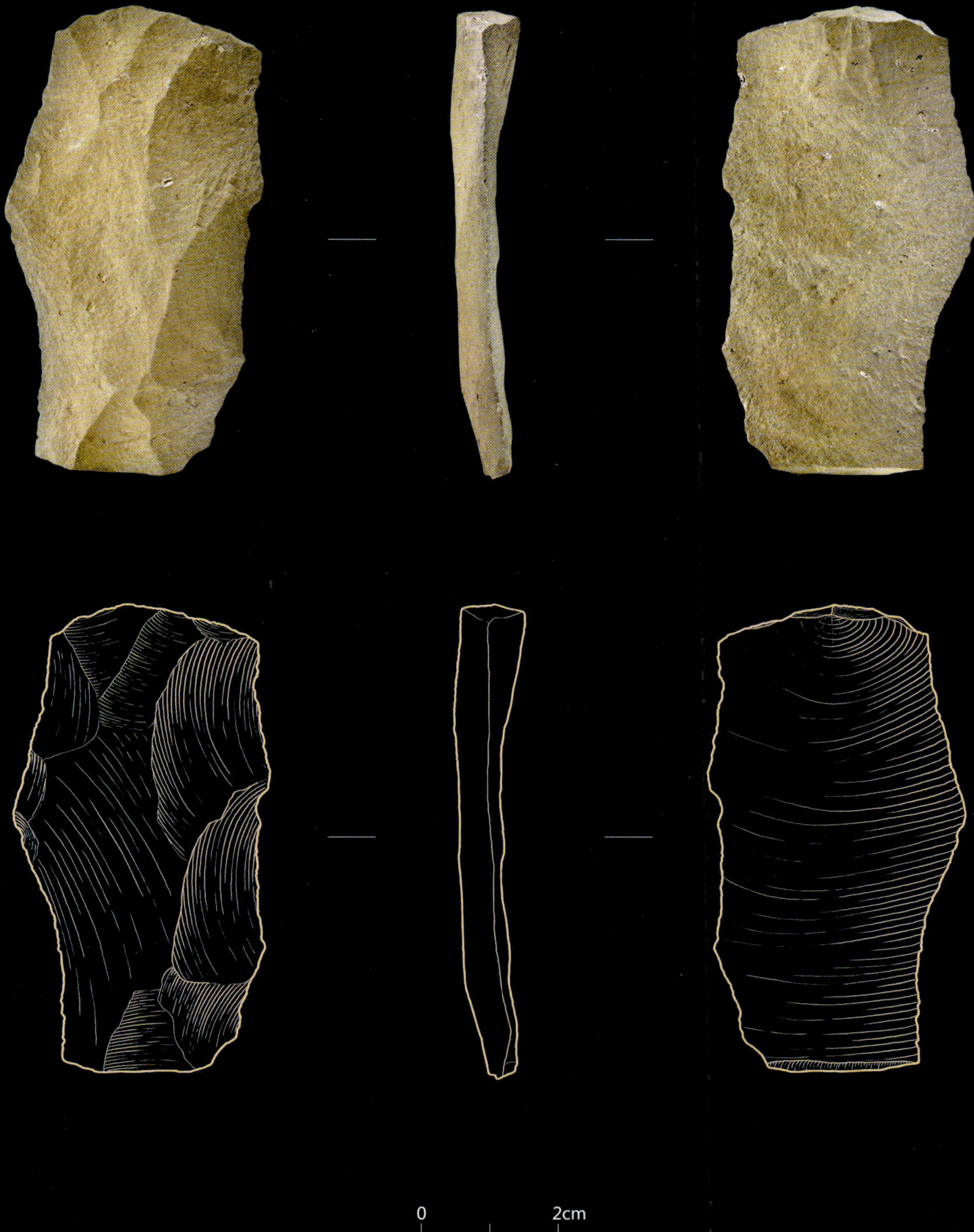

勒瓦娄哇石叶 GoJh14：286
Levallois blade 71 mm × 35 mm × 8 mm

SCRAPER

刮削器

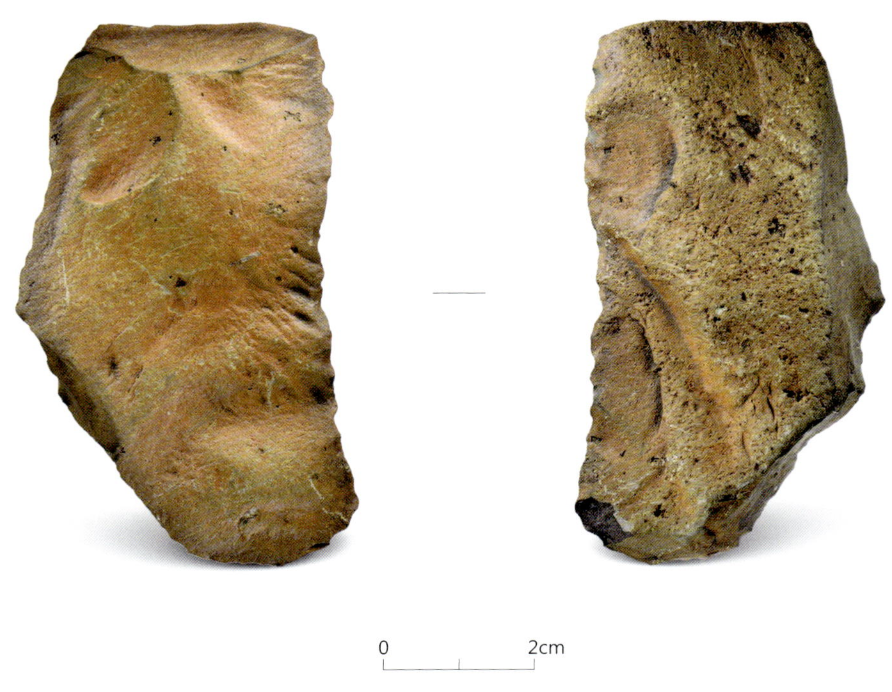

刮削器 scraper

GoJh14：322
75 mm × 43 mm × 23 mm

刮削器 scraper

GoJh14：193
66 mm × 35 mm × 10 mm

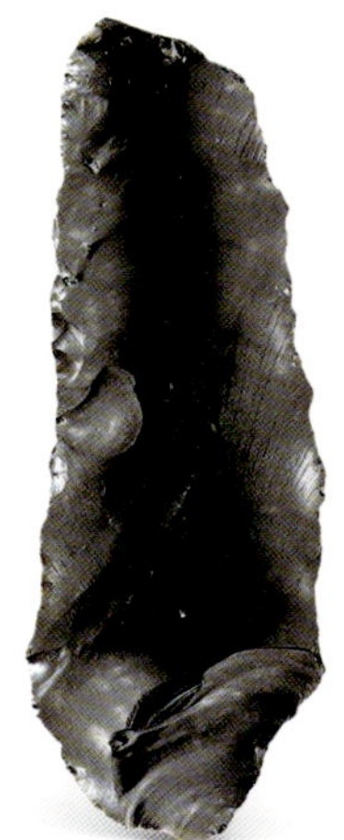

0 2cm

刮削器 scraper GoJh14 ∶ 201
59 mm × 21 mm × 7 mm

刮削器 scraper
GoJh14 ：205
24 mm × 18 mm × 5 mm

刮削器 scraper
GoJh14 ：214
35 mm × 35 mm × 8 mm

0 1cm

刮削器 scraper

GoJh14 ：237
40 mm × 18 mm × 6 mm

0 1cm

刮削器 scraper
GoJh14：306
24 mm × 13 mm × 5 mm

0 1cm

刮削器 scraper
GoJh14：305
24 mm × 14 mm × 4 mm

0 1cm

刮削器 scraper
GoJh14：333
24 mm × 21 mm × 6 mm

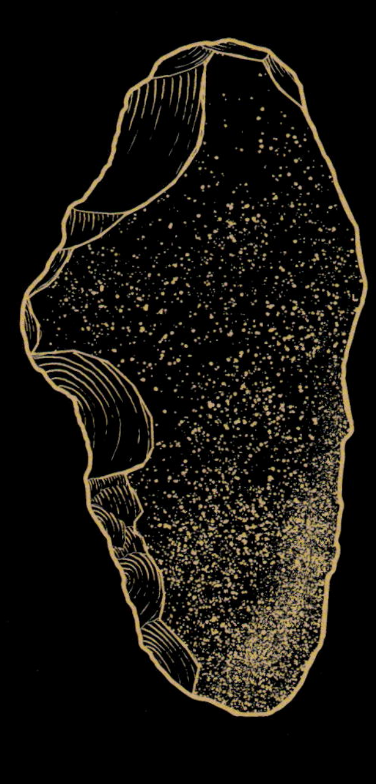

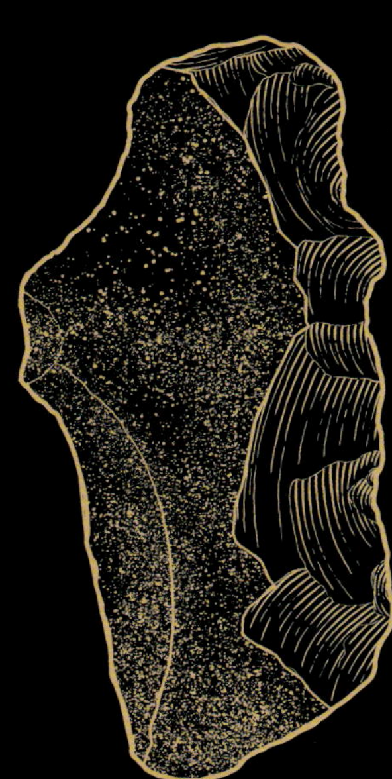

0 1cm

刮削器 scraper

GoJh14：328

39 mm × 24 mm × 9 mm

刮削器 scraper \ GoJh14 ： 334
33 mm × 35 mm × 8 mm

POINT

尖状器

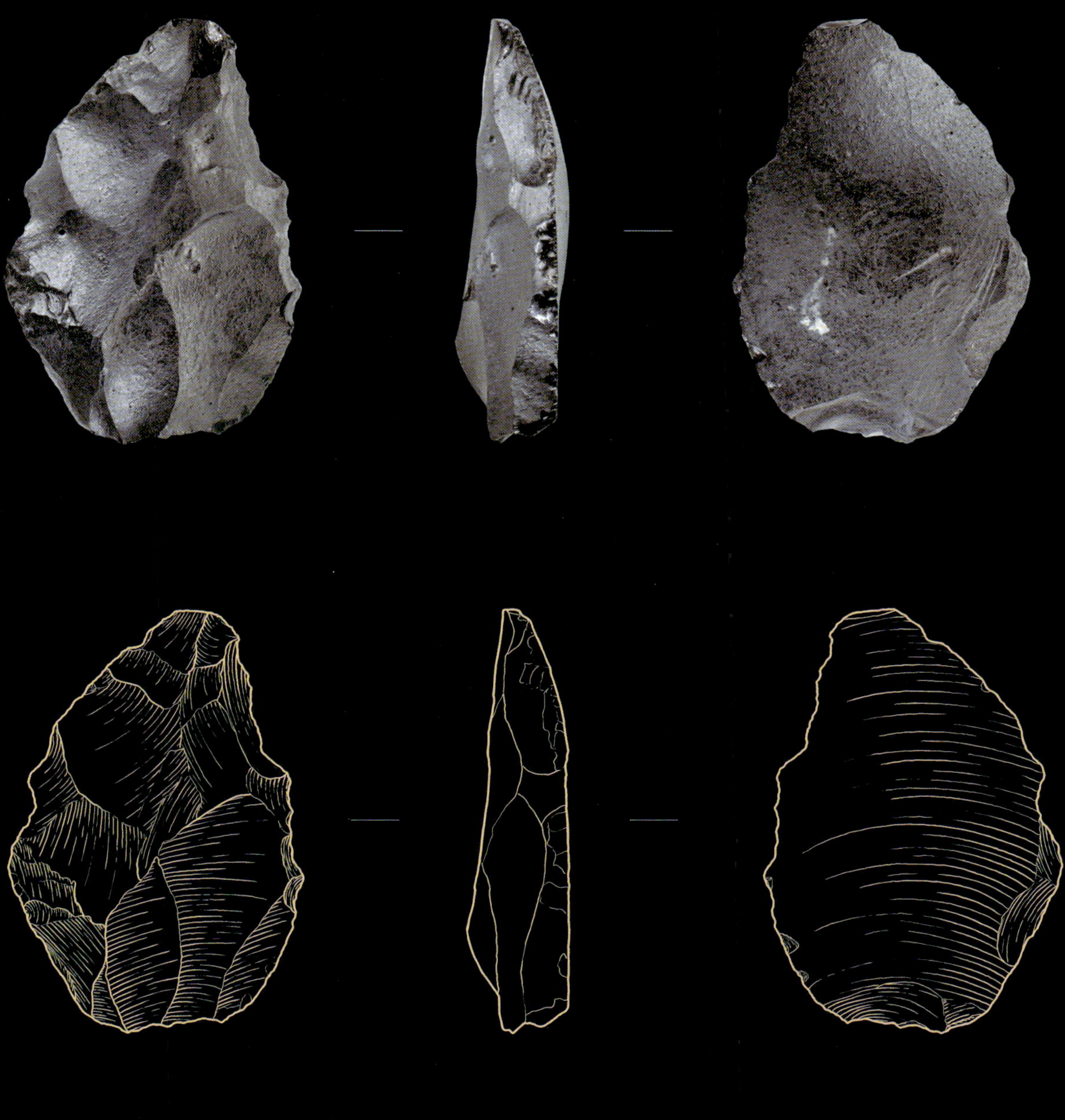

尖状器 point
GoJh14：195
32 mm × 21 mm × 7 mm

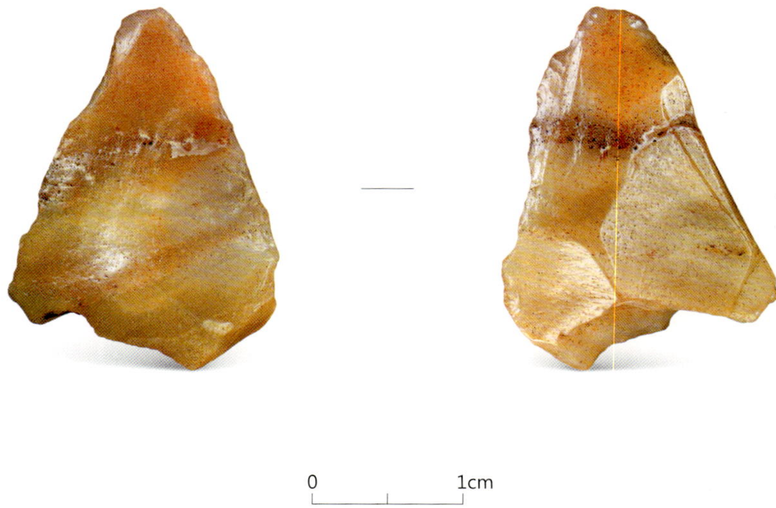

尖状器
point

GoJh14：304
25 mm × 19 mm × 8 mm

尖状器
point

GoJh14：196
28 mm × 21 mm × 7 mm

尖状器
point

GoJh14 : 222
48 mm × 28 mm × 10 mm

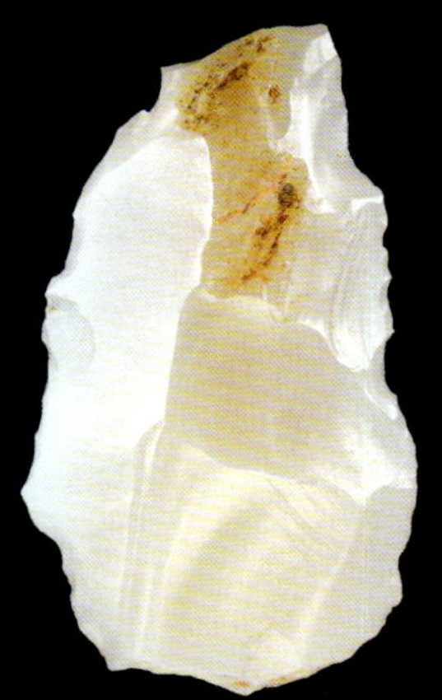

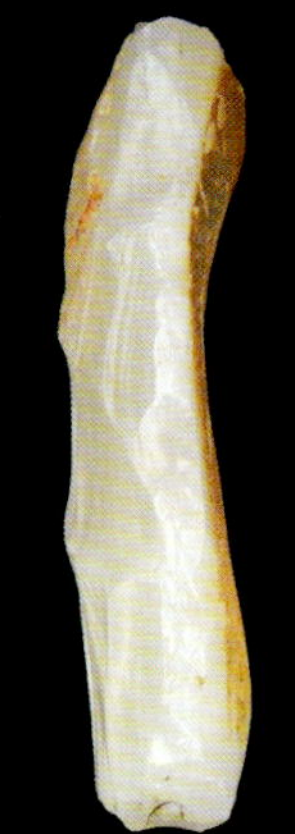

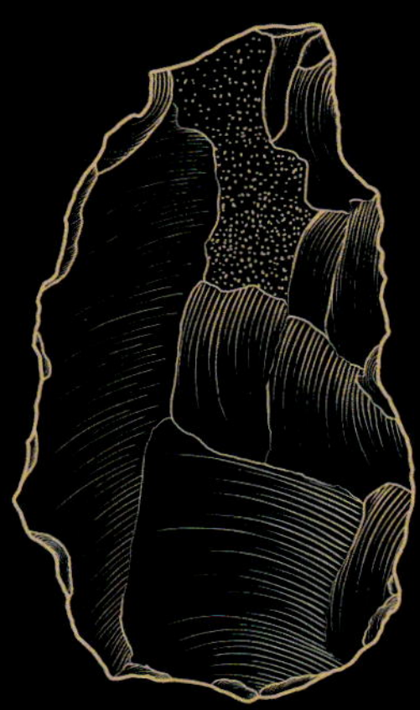

0 1cm

尖状器 point

GoJh14 ： 199
28 mm × 16 mm × 6 mm

LEVALLOIS POINT

—

勒瓦娄哇尖状器

0 2cm

勒瓦娄哇尖状器
Levallois point

GoJh14 ： 200
66 mm × 33 mm × 12 mm

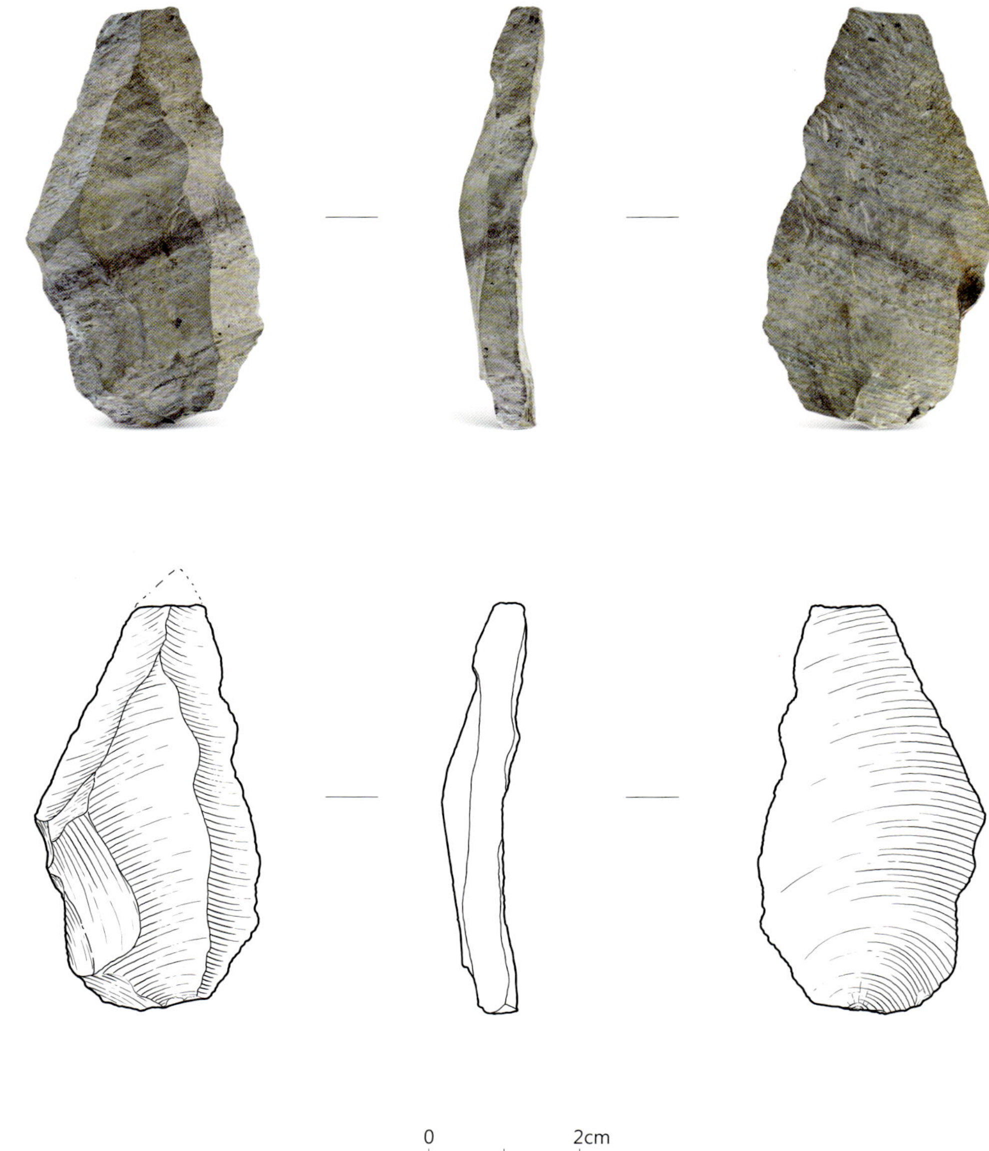

勒瓦娄哇尖状器
Levallois point

GoJh14：210
58 mm × 31 mm × 7 mm

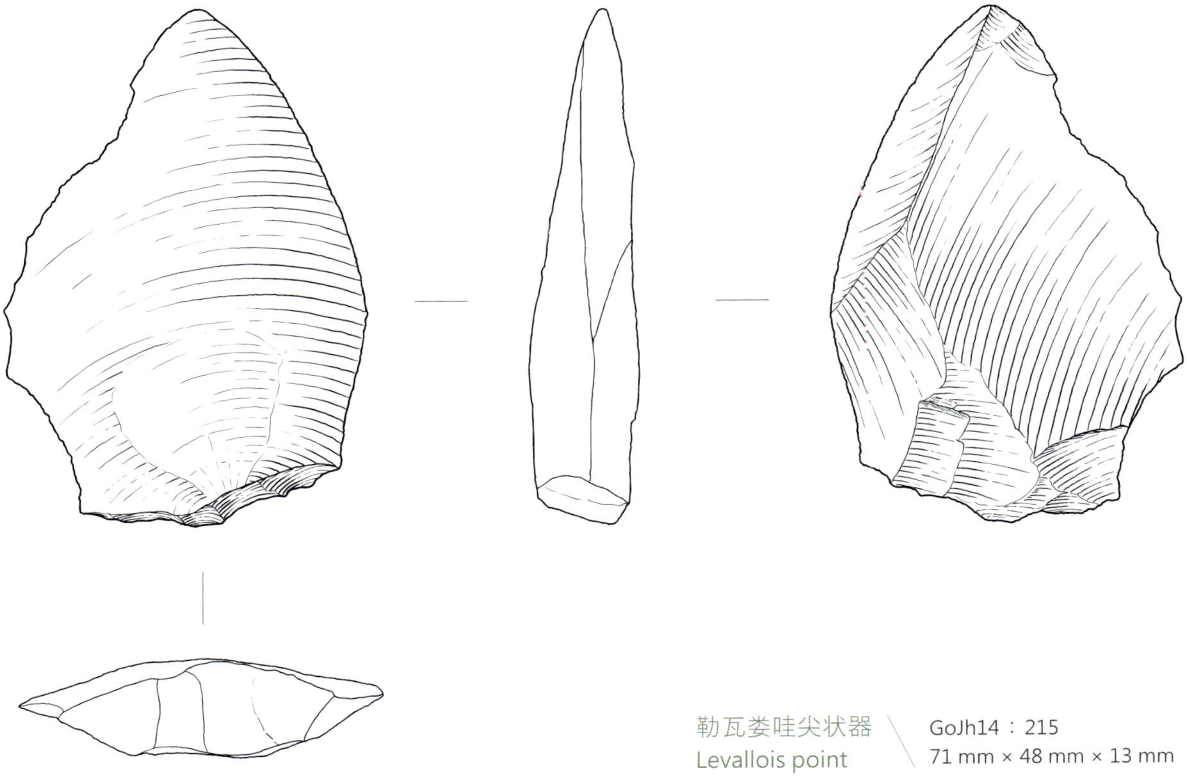

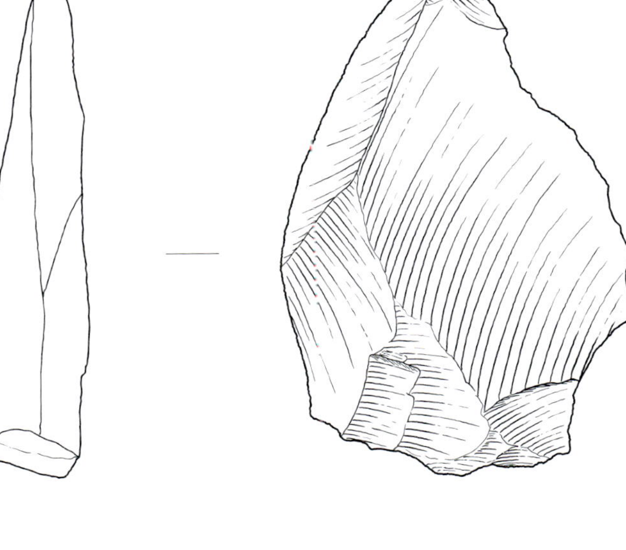

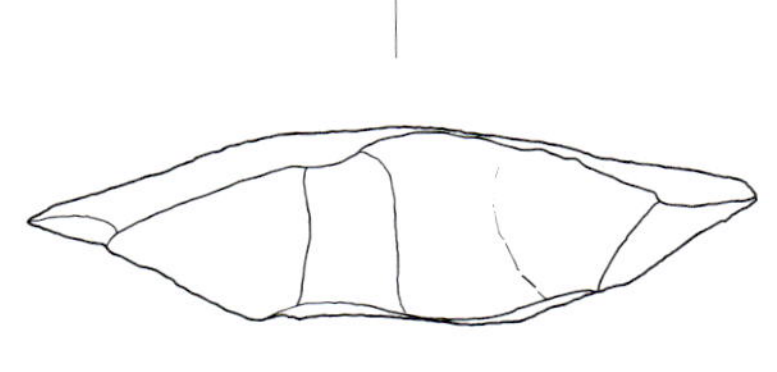

勒瓦娄哇尖状器
Levallois point

GoJh14 ：215
71 mm × 48 mm × 13 mm

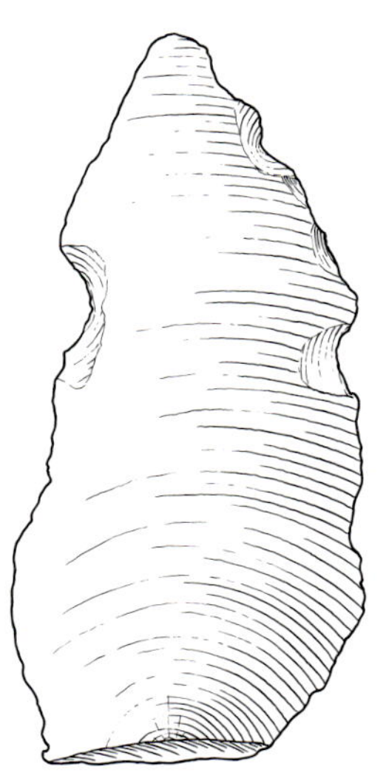
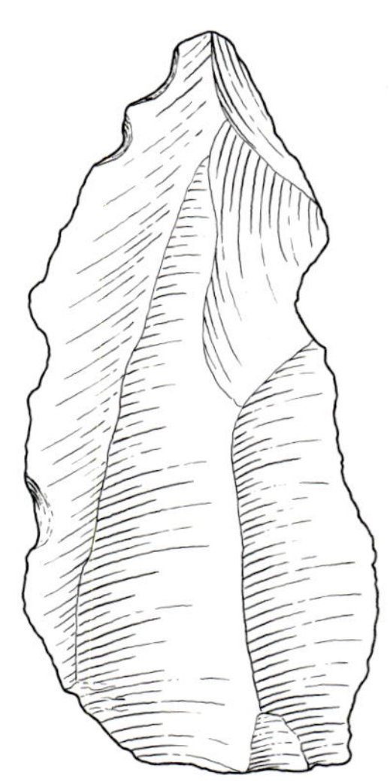

勒瓦娄哇尖状器 GoJh14：216
Levallois point 69 mm × 32 mm × 11 mm

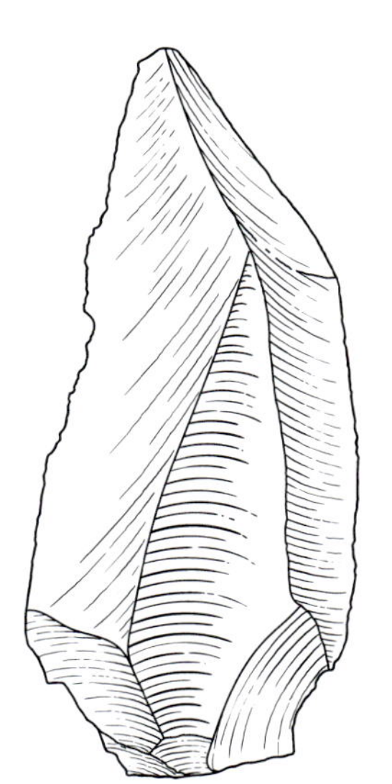
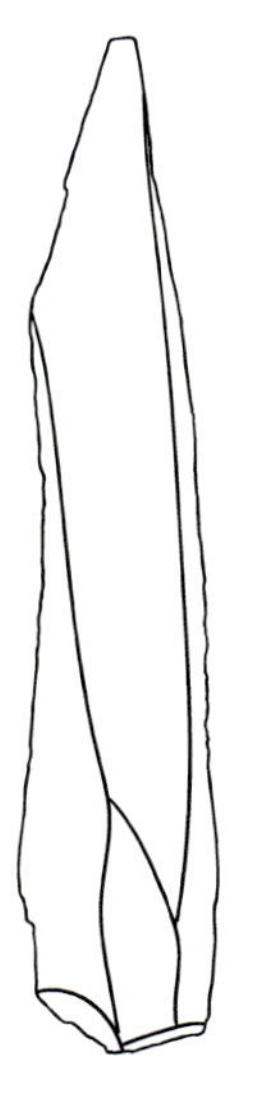
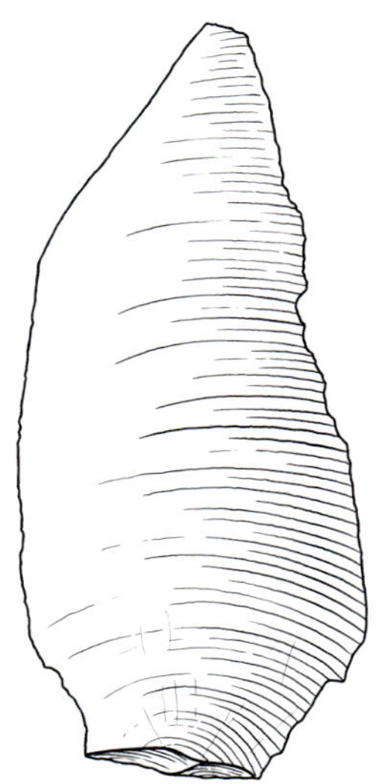

0 2cm

勒瓦娄哇尖状器
Levallois point

GoJh14 ：218
70 mm × 30 mm × 12 mm

2cm

0

勒瓦娄哇尖状器
Levallois point

GoJh14：220
92 mm × 53 mm × 14 mm

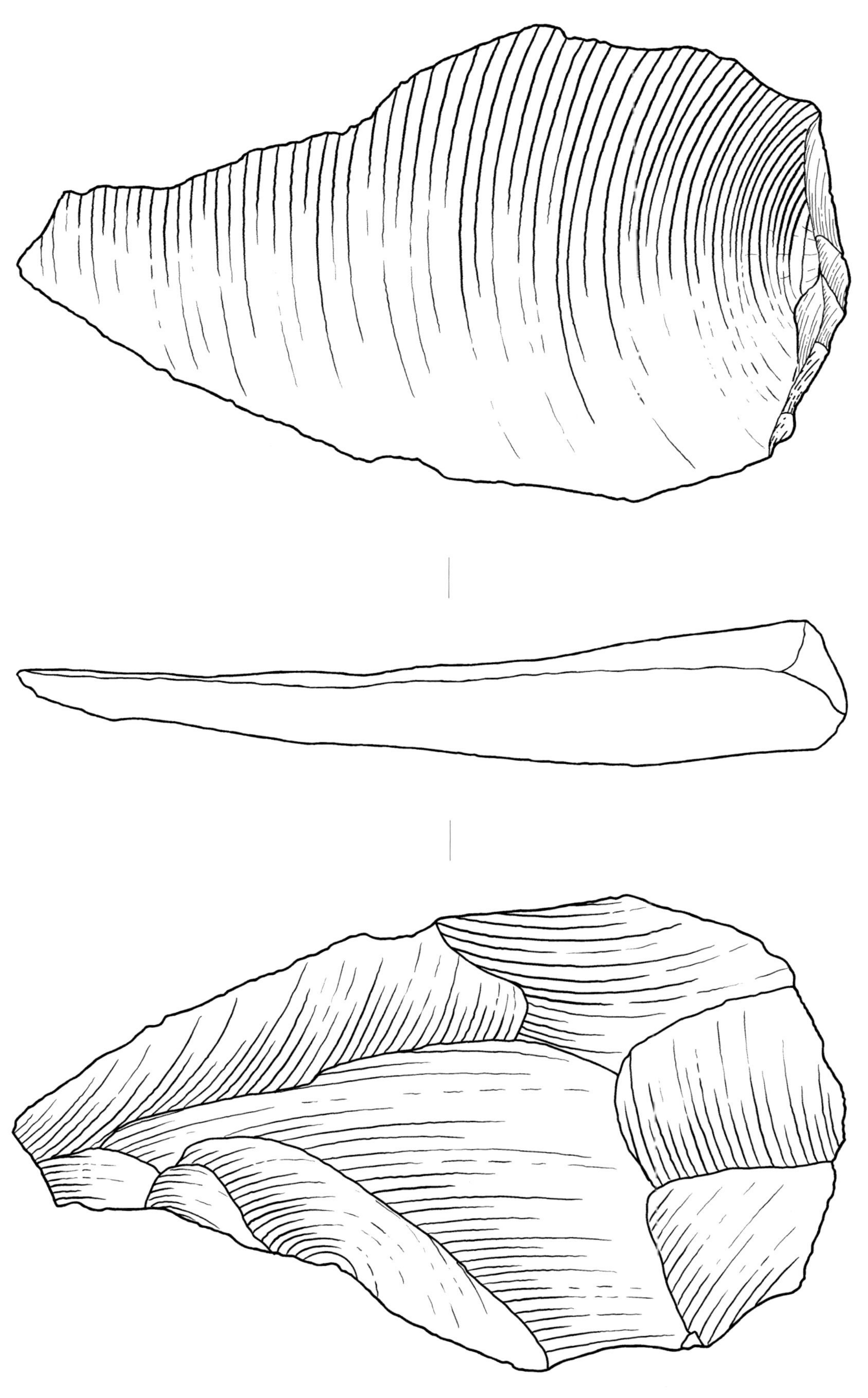

勒瓦娄哇尖状器
Levallois point

GoJh14：230
91 mm × 50 mm × 15 mm

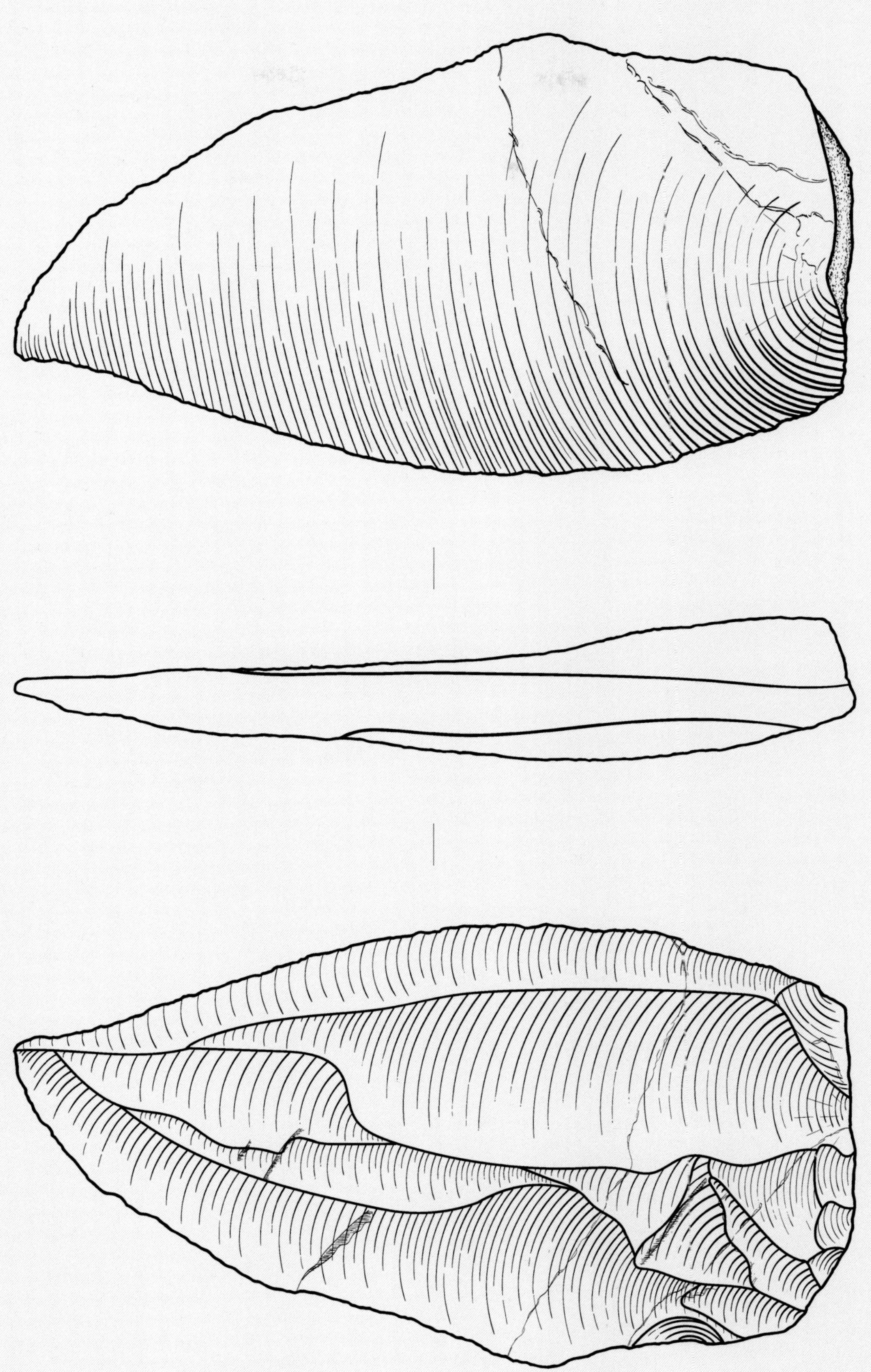

勒瓦娄哇尖状器
Levallois point

GoJh14：235
80 mm × 35 mm × 10 mm

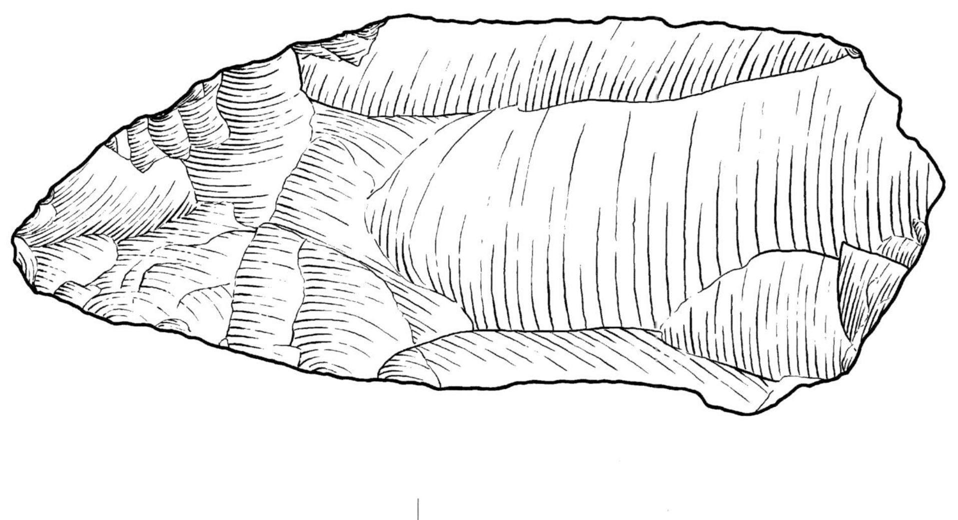

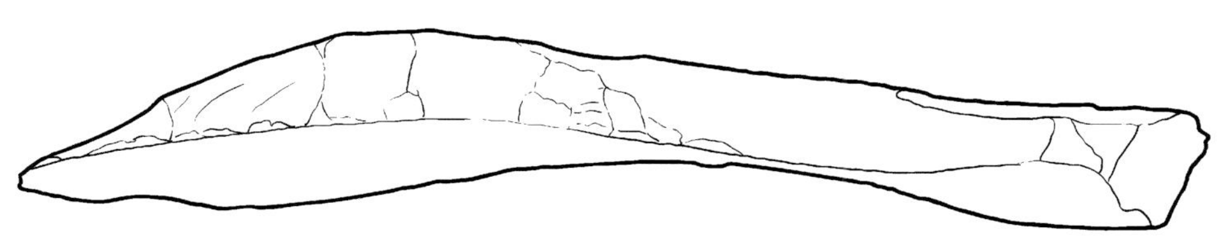

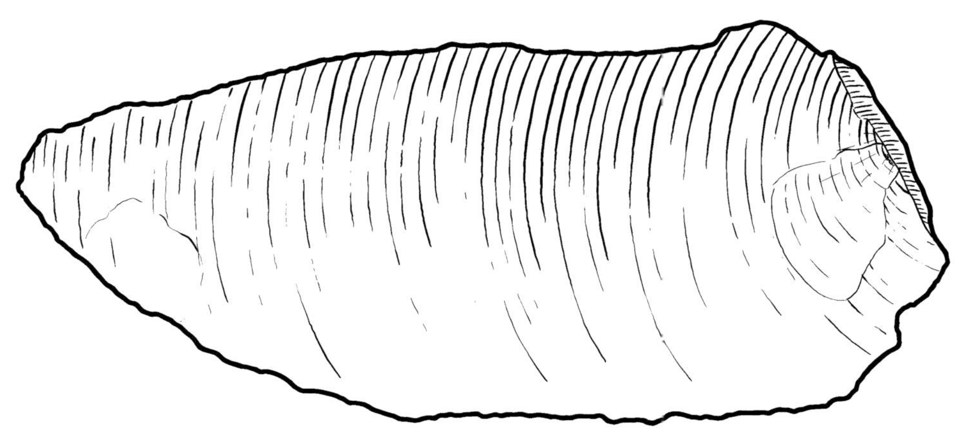

勒瓦娄哇尖状器
Levallois point

GoJh14：268
89 mm × 50 mm × 12 mm

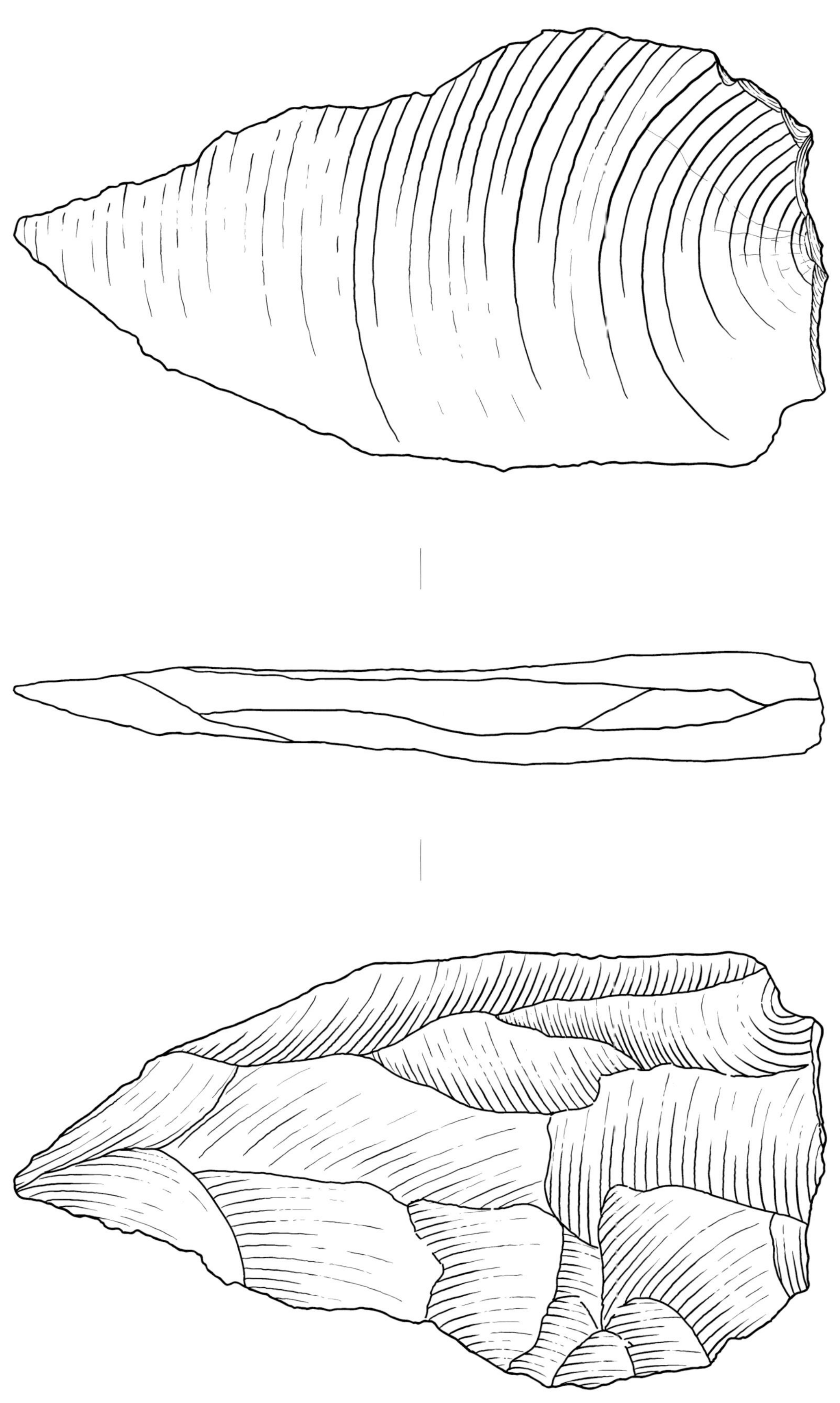

勒瓦娄哇尖状器　GoJh14：269
Levallois point　86 mm × 48 mm × 13 mm

勒瓦娄哇尖状器
Levallois point

GoJh14：270
112 mm × 67 mm × 21 mm

勒瓦娄哇尖状器 \ GoJh14：271
Levallois point \ 97 mm × 61 mm × 17 mm

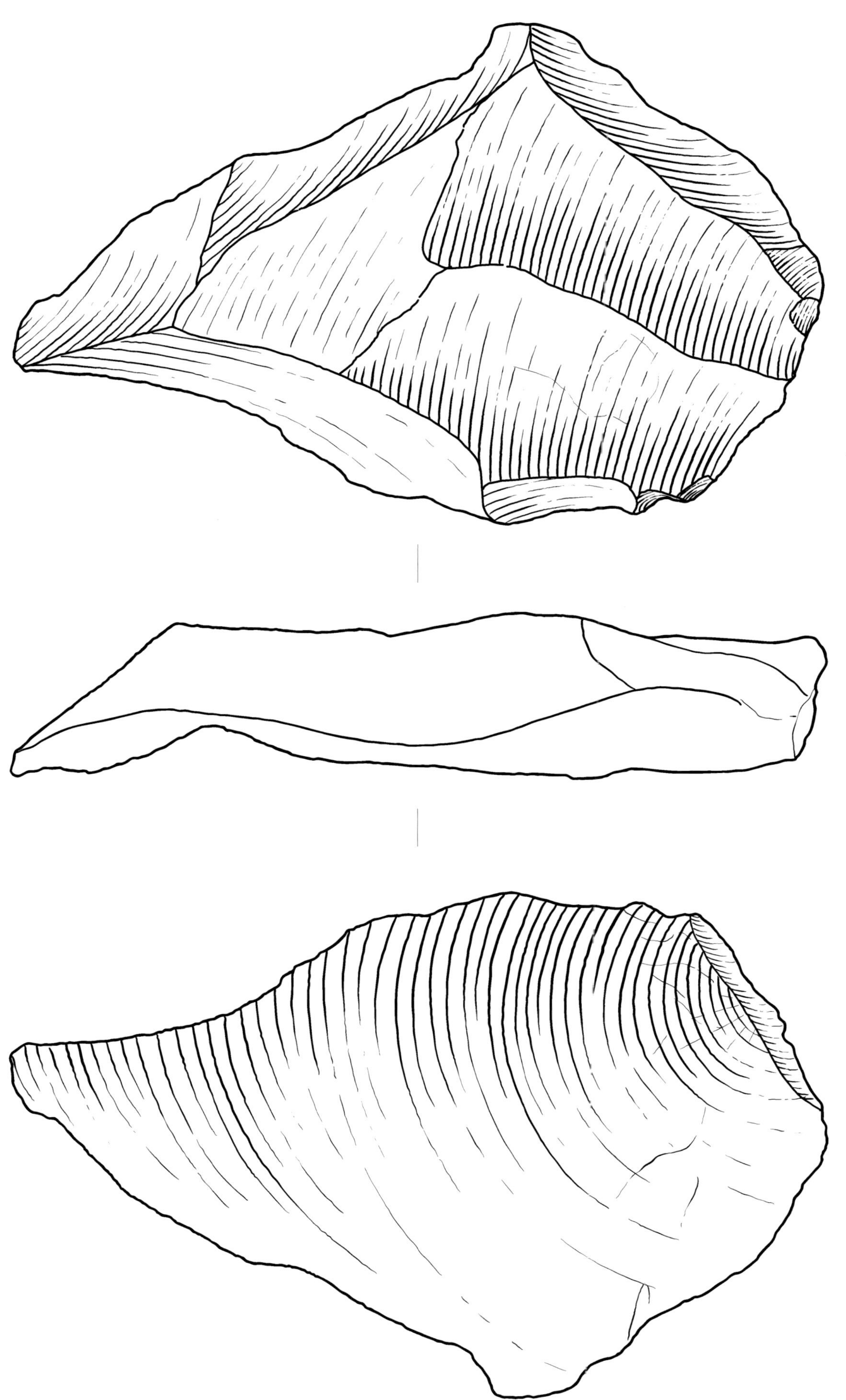

勒瓦娄哇尖状器
Levallois point

GoJh14 ：278
82 mm × 41 mm × 14 mm

勒瓦娄哇尖状器
Levallois point

GoJh14 ：273
71 mm × 48 mm × 12 mm

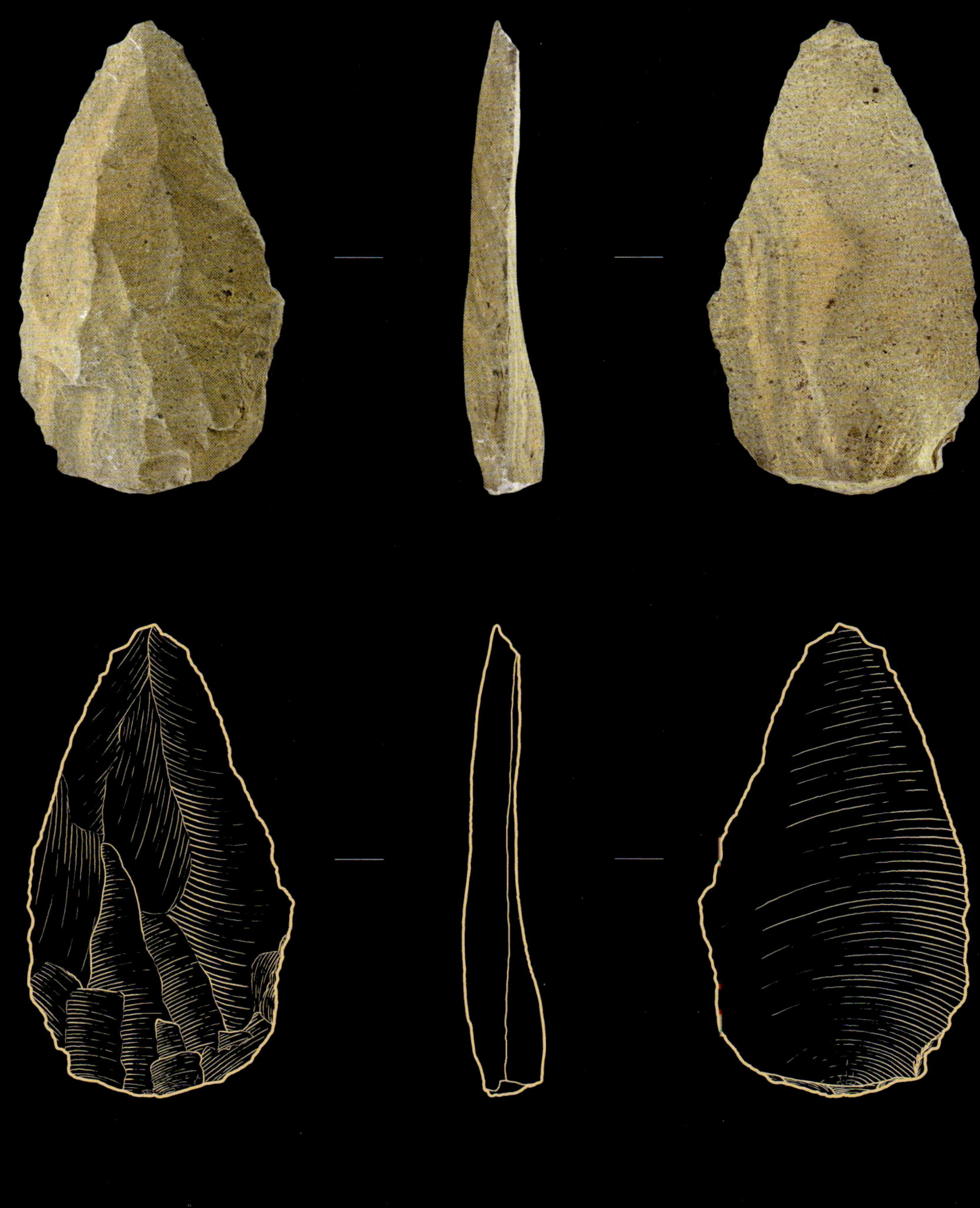

0 2cm

勒瓦娄哇尖状器 Levallois point

GoJh14 ： 291
71 mm × 40 mm × 10 mm

2cm

0

勒瓦娄哇尖状器 ╲ GoJh14：323
Levallois point ╲ 91 mm × 58 mm × 11 mm

勒瓦娄哇尖状器
Levallois point

GoJh14：335
95 mm × 51 mm × 23 mm

OTHER STONE ARTIFACTS

其他

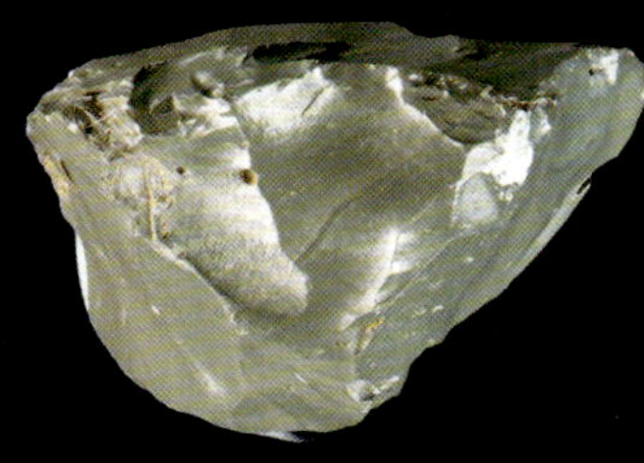

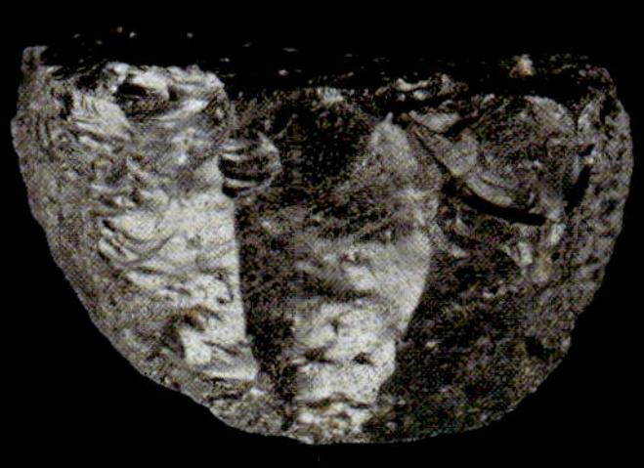

0 1cm

0 1cm

石核 \ GoJh14：307
core 15 mm × 21 mm × 22 mm

细石核 \ GoJh14：327
microblade core 10 mm × 14 mm × 12 mm

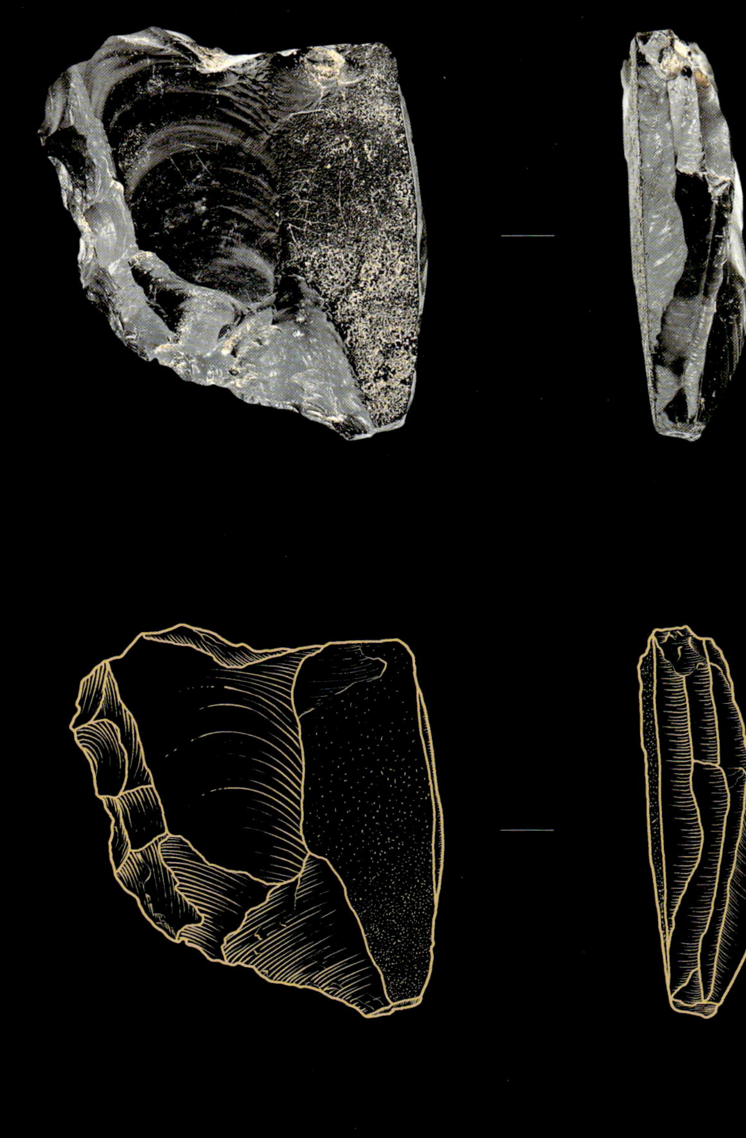

0 1cm

细石核
microblade core

GoJh14：229
19 mm × 18 mm × 3 mm

0 2cm

钻器 GoJh14：339
borer 59 mm × 34 mm × 8 mm

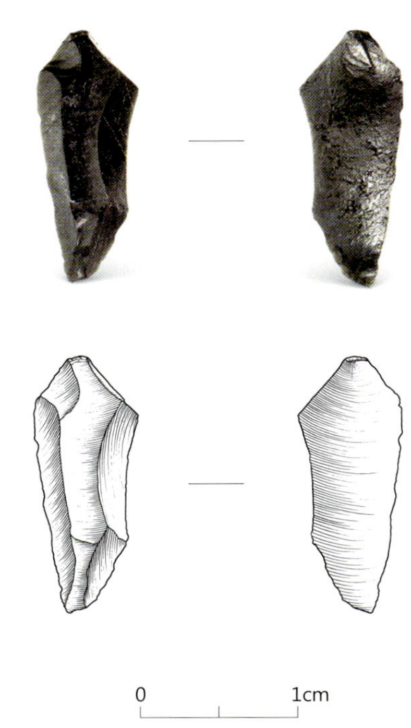

0 1cm

小石叶 bladelet GoJh14：194
17 mm × 7 mm × 4 mm

0 2cm

削片 spall GoJh14：223
49 mm × 24 mm × 12 mm

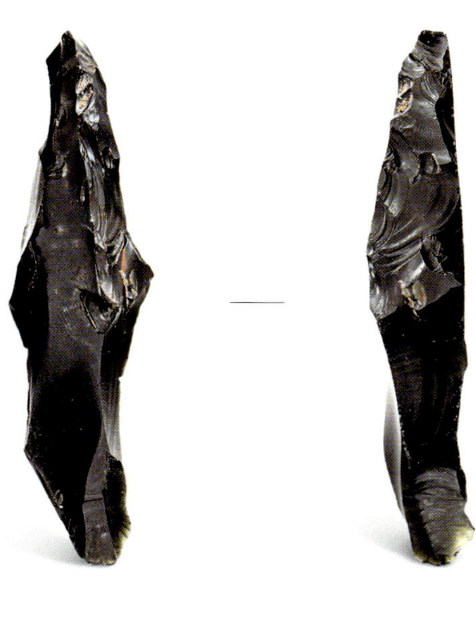

0 1cm

削片 spall GoJh14：228
34 mm × 9 mm × 6 mm

0 1cm

小石叶 bladelet GoJh14：226
16 mm × 8 mm × 2 mm

琢背小刀 GoJh14：332
backed knife 21 mm × 7 mm × 7 mm

琢背小刀 GoJh14：227
backed knife 19 mm × 6 mm × 4 mm

0 2cm

端刮器
endscraper

GoJh14：313
65 mm × 43 mm × 21 mm

0 2cm

手斧
hand-axe

GoJh14：301
127 mm × 89 mm × 48 mm

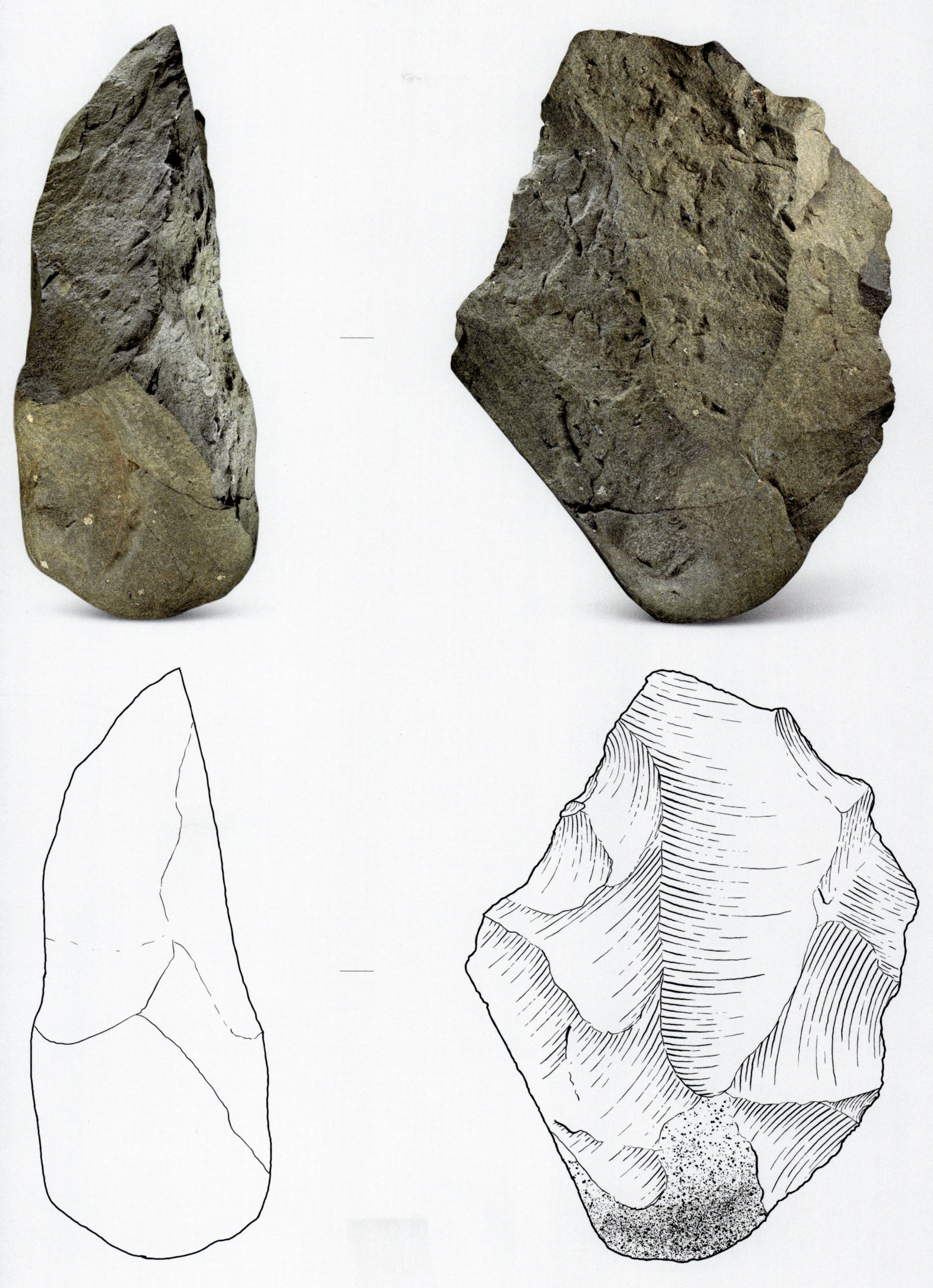

0 2cm

手斧 GoJh14：219
hand-axe 178 mm × 113 mm × 61 mm

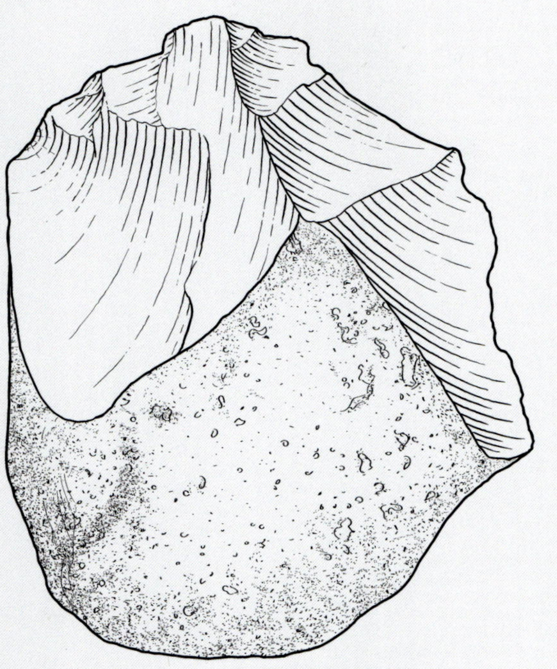

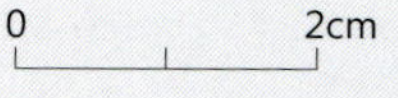

砍砸器 chopper

GoJh14：309
89 mm × 72 mm × 32 mm

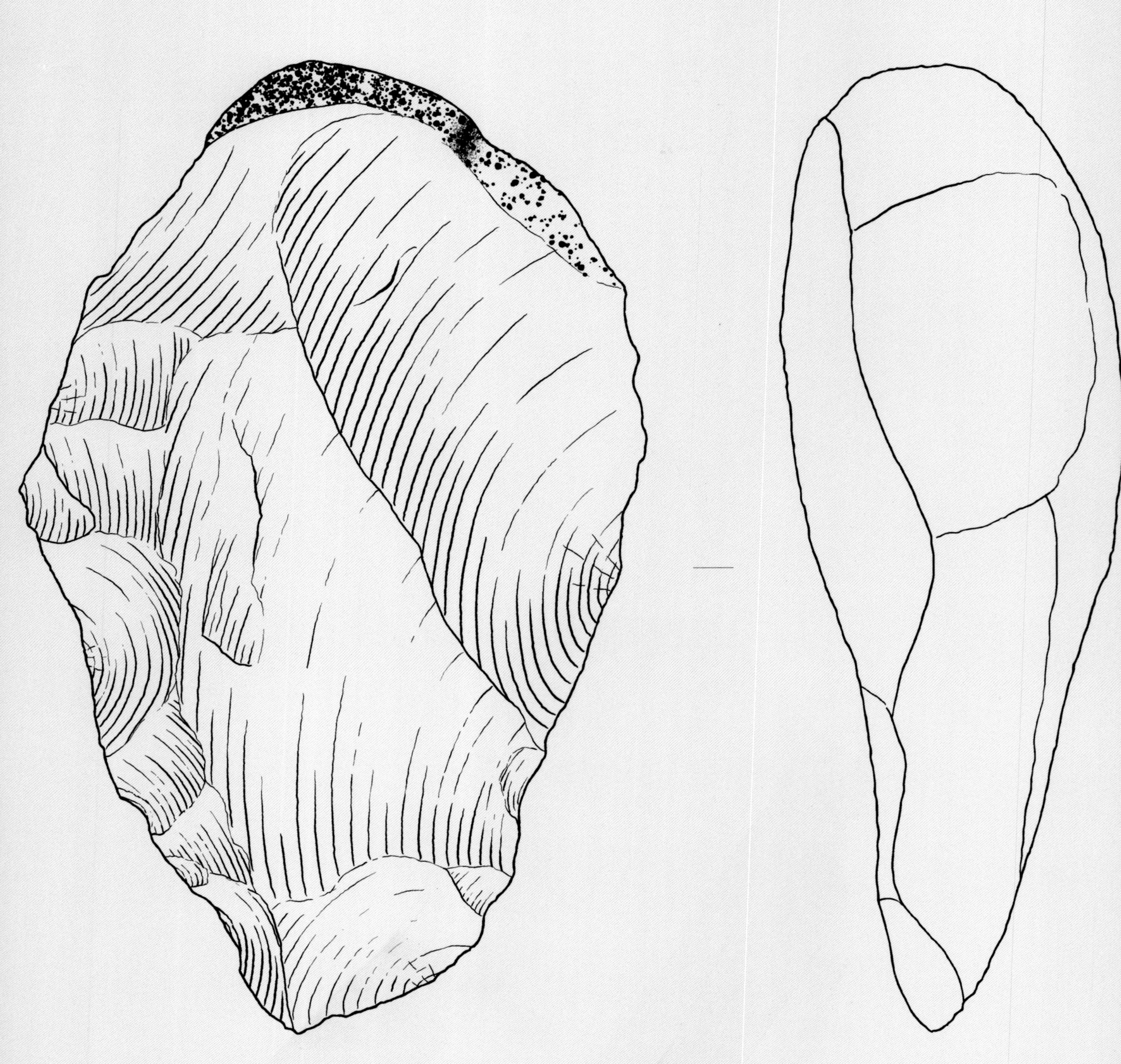

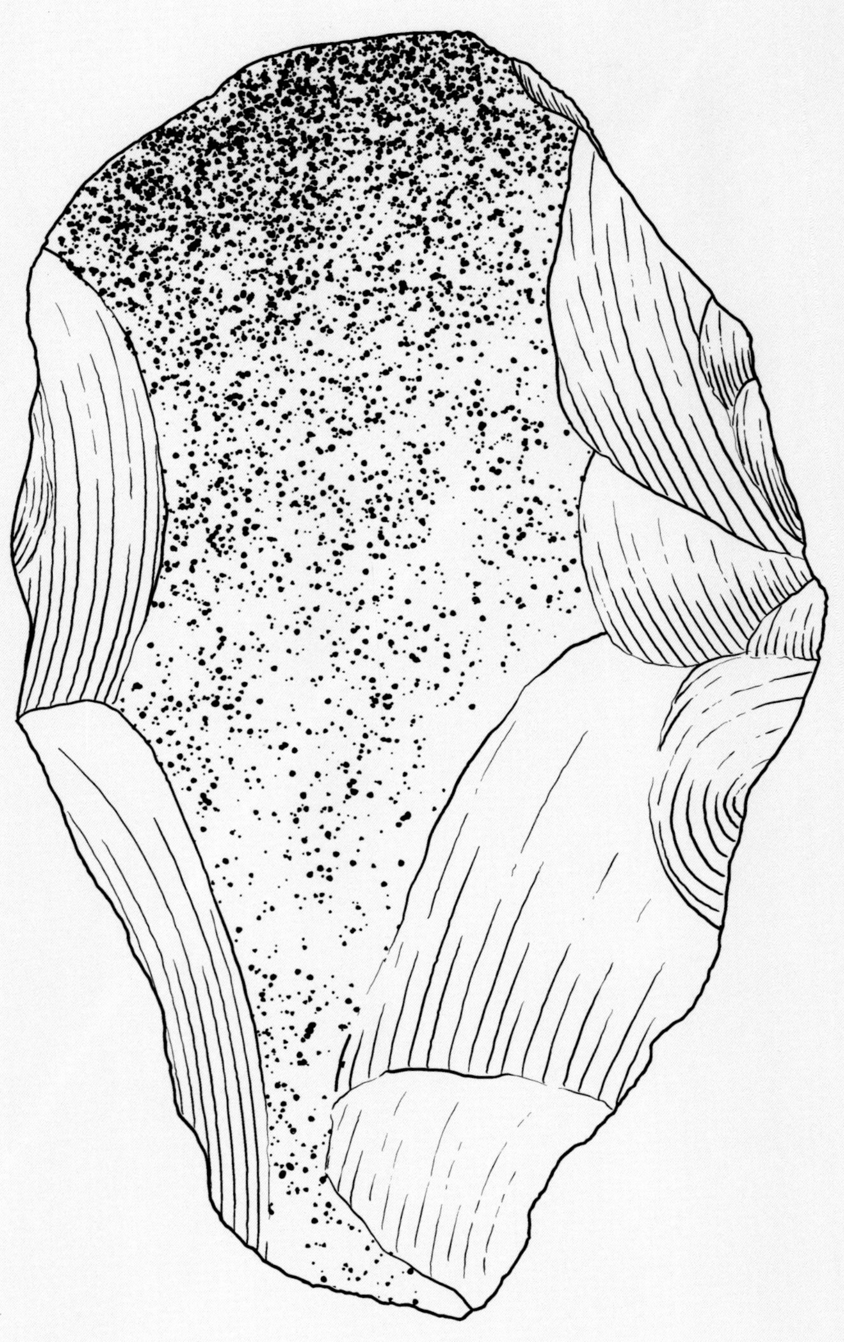

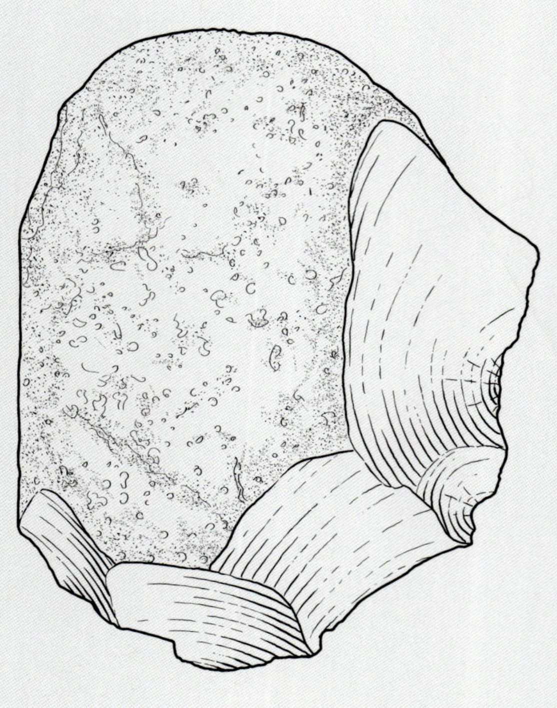
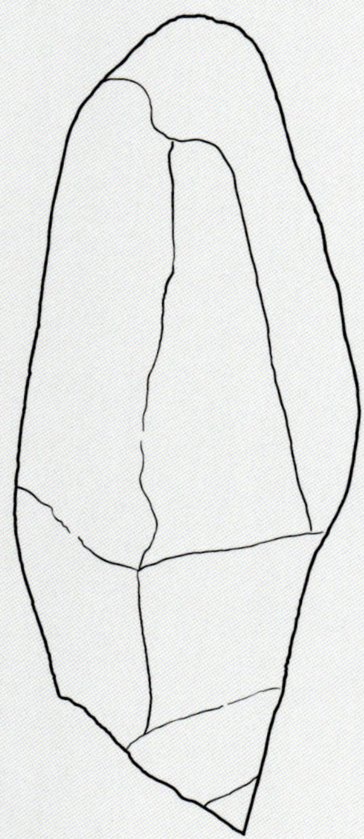

手镐 pick

GoJh14：302
180 mm × 98 mm × 70 mm

考古队员采访录

中肯联合考古队中方现场负责人赵清坡说:“在我们来之前，还没有中国做旧石器、古人类考古的人到这里，主要就是一些欧美学者在做工作。之前我们拿不到一手资料，我们能参考、引用的仅限于文献。旧石器考古是没有国界之分的。人类的摇篮就在我们脚下，我们能在这里工作真的是很荣幸。我们和肯尼亚的合作是非常好的，我们带着新的设备、技术和方法来到这里，他们有很好的旧石器考古领域的资源，我们就可以很好地结合起来，开展合作，双方互利互惠。现在国家也支持，所以我们要走出来做这件事情。”

中方考古队员娄文台说:“我觉得跟肯方工作人员的相处非常愉快，他们对我们的到来非常热情。在跟他们一块工作的过程中，我学到了很多。”

中方考古队员彭胜蓝说:“在来肯尼亚之前，会觉得这里可能比较贫瘠。来到这里之后觉得这片土地非常富饶。大家平常每天在工地都是伴随着音乐，欢声笑语的。但肯方队员在工作中非常认真，平时有一些专业方面的问题会很积极地跟我们交流。我们会经常交流一些斯瓦西里语和中文，大家会互相学习。”

肯方考古队员菲斯・万布阿说:“我是 2017 年就加入项目的成员，中方队员对我们的帮助很大，从中方队员那里我了解到了中国考古界的近况，还了解到摄影测量法可以为石器进行三维建模。”

肯方考古队员帕特里克・尼亚加提到:“我很高兴加入这个项目，能和中国考古队员一起工作感觉非常棒。他们帮助我们认识人类起源以及人类打制石器技术的演化，我还学到了一些关于无人机的知识，中方队员教我如何使用无人机进行航拍。我希望未来能有更多机会和他们一起工作。”

肯方考古队员瑞贝卡·穆索尼说：“一开始我对中国考古学一无所知，当我参观了他们的驻地，了解他们整理石器的方法和技术，使用三维扫描仪获得石器三维模型，我很钦佩。现在我和他们一起工作，看到他们所做的事情以及我们的合作，我很受鼓舞。”

中肯旧石器联合考古项目肯方负责人乔布·基比表示：“在这里进行考古发掘工作，遇到比较大的困难就是很多人不知道我们在挖什么，有人以为我们在挖钻石。我们雇用当地工人，教他们关于石器的知识，这样他们也能了解和书写人类历史，因为这段历史就在他们身边。中肯两国专家在考古学领域的合作意义重大，中方带来了新的技术，我们用这些技术标记石器位置和地形，以寻找发掘地点。他们经常为肯方队员提供各种培训，比如无人机航拍、石器摄影和三维扫描等。我们在这里考古是因为我们的祖先曾在这片土地上生活，我们与中国考古队员合作，他们帮助我们书写人类起源篇章，去探寻人类是如何进化和发展的，这是具有世界意义的事，因为这事关人类历史。我们有共同的历史，这让我们团结在一起。”

INTERVIEW

Zhao Qingpo, leading member of the Sino-Kenya joint archaeological team: "Before we came here, no Chinese Paleolithic or paleoanthropological team had ever been to this area. Scholars from Europe and the U.S. have been doing researches here in the past. At that time, we couldn't get first-hand materials, what we could refer to and cite were limited to documents and literatures. Paleolithic archaeology has no national boundaries. The cradle of humanity lies right beneath our feet, and it's truly an honor to work here. Our collaboration with National Museums of Kenya is excellent. We bring new equipment, technologies, and methods, while they possess valuable resources in Paleolithic archaeology. Together, we can integrate well and collaborate for mutual benefits. With the support of our respective mother country, it's essential for us to go outside and to engage in this endeavor.

Lou Wentai, member of the Sino-Kenya joint archaeological team: "I feel very happy to get along with the Kenya staff, they are very enthusiastic about our arrival. I learned a lot when working with them."

Peng Shenglan, member of the Sino-Kenya joint archaeological team: "Before I came to Kenya, I thought it's poor and less developed. But when I arrive, I feel this land is rich in resources. The archaeological excavation is always accompanied by music. Our Kenyan workmates are always in good moods and dedicated to their work. They always actively communicate with us about professional knowledge. We learn languages from each other, like Swahili and Chinese."

Faith Wambua, research fellow at National Museums of Kenya: "I took part in this project in 2017. Chinese archaeologists have been helpful to us by giving us a chance to know what happens in China. One of the thing that I have learned is that photogrammetry can be used to create 3D model for stone tools."

Patrick Nyaga, collection manager of National Museums of Kenya: "I am very happy to join this project, and it feels great to work with our China colleagues. They help us understand the origins of human beings and evolution of lithic technology. I have learned how to use drones for aerial photography from them. I hope to have more opportunities to work with them in future."

Rebecca Muthoni, staff at the Earth Sciences Department of National Museums of Kenya: "At first, I didn't know anything of archaeology in China. Then I visited their station and understood their methods and techniques. I was really impressed that they used 3D Scanner to create 3D models of stone tools. Now working with them and seeing what they are doing and what we do together, it's encouraging."

Job Kibii, leading member of the Sino-Kenya joint archaeological team: "In this project, one of the challenges is that local people didn't know what we are doing. There are people who thought maybe we are mining diamonds. We have employed them in this project. Teach them what those stone tools are, so that they can start knowing and writing the history of mankind, in their backyard. The cooperation between Chinese and Kenyan experts in the field of archaeology is of great significance. Chinese collaborators have brought new technologies, and we used these technologies to mark the positions of stone tools in order to find new excavation sites. We conduct archaeology here because our ancestors have lived here. We have Chinese collaborators in this project. They are helping to write the chapters of how humans came about, how humans developed. This is a matter of world significance, because it concerns human history. That unites us, because we know we have a common history."

后 记

中肯旧石器联合考古项目自 2017 年开始，已进行四年，我是唯一全程参与项目的成员。在 2017 年项目刚启动时，院领导安排我具体操办与肯方沟通、项目申报、队员出国手续等事宜。第一年可以说是摸着石头过河，没有一点经验可言，往往是在后两年看似很简单的某一个程序，有可能都要跑好几个地方协调办理。毕竟 2017 年，我们也是第一次代表河南省文物考古研究院到非洲开展旧石器考古发掘工作，毫无经验可以借鉴。好在第一年项目手续办理过程中积累了大量经验，后续三次办理相关手续时，可谓轻车熟路。

后续三次赴肯尼亚，我作为现场负责人，除了业务工作外，还要统筹考虑队员们的吃穿住行和安全，尤其 2018 年，身份突然的转换，对我来说是挑战也是机遇。2023 年，其他三位中方队员都是第一次来到肯尼亚，见到遍地的精美石器很是兴奋，完全再现了我初到肯尼亚的情形。

赤道贯穿肯尼亚中部，这里天气炎热，正午时分考古队员仍穿梭在针刺密布的杂树丛中，头顶炎炎烈日，脚踩滚烫沙石，寻找新的旧石器地点。在肯尼亚的考古调查较为艰苦，考古调查的区域大多位于人烟稀少的地区，低矮灌木丛生，实地调查时须非常小心谨慎。和国内进行旧石器考古调查不同，在肯尼亚，我们不得不步行踏查，用脚丈量每一寸土地，一是因为荒野中没有路，车开不了；二是这里考古地点比较密集，开车很容易错过重要线索。调查时，GPS 是必须要携带的设备，一是为了记录走过的路线，避免以后重复调查；二是为了防止迷路。肯尼亚野外紫外线非常强烈，晒伤晒黑已是考古队员的家常便饭。饮食条件也不容乐观，日常餐食就是肯尼亚当地便餐或者榨菜等方便食品。队员们苦中作乐，在工作之余偶尔煮奶茶，或利用现有食材自己下厨再加工，改善伙食。虽然条件艰苦，但是在调查过程中丰富的发现，能瞬间冲淡疲惫的身心，取而代之的是发现遗物的兴奋，偶尔发现野生仙人掌果也是工作中难得的乐趣。发现旧石器地点后，考古队员们就会各自忙碌起来，写石器标签，拍摄现场及周边地貌照片，记录发现地点坐标等，队员们分工明确，井然有序。

2017 年，在肯尼亚工作期间，我们有幸受到肯尼亚前总统莫伊先生的接见。到现在我还依然清晰地记得，当时我与总统先生握手时，老先生嗓音浑厚，缓慢说道:“我非常喜欢中国，还经常到中国上海。”

在肯尼亚工作四个年度，每次初到或离开肯尼亚时，中方队员们都会收到我国驻肯尼亚大使馆的邀请，每当我走进大门的那一刻，就会有种漂泊在外终于到家的安全感。原中国驻肯尼亚大使刘显法、张罡、刘震宇、崔卿、李美璇等诸位领导对我们的工作给予了大力支持，同在巴林戈地区的中方企业的韩珂、康国栋两位先生在日常生活方面给予我们很多帮助。2019、2023 年，河南省文物局张慧明副局长、王瑞琴处长不远万里率团赴博戈里亚湖遗址考古工地慰问指导，并与肯尼亚国家博物馆领导交流座谈。新华社、中央电视台、《中国日报》等驻肯尼亚的媒体对我们的工作也非常关注，进行了大量宣传报道。受新华社应强、李文飞、代贺等先生邀请，2023 年野外工作结束之际，考古队还有幸到新华社非洲总分社交流座谈。

书中遗址及发掘现场照片由赵清坡、娄文台、顾雪军和乔布 · 基比共同拍摄，石制品照片由赵清坡拍摄，石制品线图由赵清坡和彭胜蓝绘制。中国国家文物局、河南省文物局、河南省文物考古研究院、洛阳市考古研究院、中国驻肯尼亚大使馆、肯尼亚国家博物馆等单位领导，两位中肯联合考古项目主任李占扬教授（2017 年、2018 年）、魏兴涛研究员（2019 年、2023 年），两位肯方项目负责人乔布 · 基比、伊曼纽尔 · 恩迪玛，以及刘海旺院长、玛丽 · 吉昆古馆长对联合考古项目给予大力支持。谨向上述各位领导以及参与中肯联合考古项目的工作者致以诚挚谢意。

赵清坡

2024 年 4 月 15 日

POSTSCRIPT

The Sino-Kenya Paleolithic Archaeological Project has been ongoing since 2017, marking four years of continuous work. As the sole member who participated in every season, I was responsible for handling the project application and the procedures for team members traveling abroad in 2017. In the first year, I felt like I was "crossing the river by feeling the stones," as the Chinese saying goes. Representing the Henan Provincial Institute of Cultural Heritage and Archaeology, we were conducting Paleolithic archaeological excavations in Africa for the first time, with no prior experience. Fortunately, our efforts in the first year yielded significant insights, which greatly benefited our work in the subsequent years.

During the subsequent three seasons in Kenya, as the field manager, I was responsible for arranging the accommodation and transportation for our team, overseeing operational work, and ensuring the safety of the team members. In 2023, my colleagues were thrilled to see the exquisite lithic artifacts scattered across the excavation and survey sites in Kenya, reminiscent of the excitement I felt upon my first arrival. Kenya, straddled by the equator, experiences extreme heat. Despite the harsh midday sun, our members diligently searched for new sites, navigating through thorny overgrowth, with the sun beating down on them and their feet treading on hot sand and gravel. Archaeological investigations in Kenya are particularly challenging as most survey areas are sparsely populated with low shrubs. These field surveys demand great care and attention. Unlike Paleolithic surveys in China, in Kenya, we had to conduct thorough, on-foot investigations, meticulously examining every inch of the land. Driving was not an option due to the lack of roads in the wilderness and the high density of archaeological sites, which made it easy to miss important clues while driving. GPS devices were essential during the survey to record our routes, avoid repetition in the future, and prevent getting lost.

The ultraviolet ray in Kenya are extremely strong, and sunburn and tanning have become commonplace for our team members. The food conditions are also less than ideal, with daily meals consisting of local lunches or convenient foods like pickled vegetables. The team found joy amidst the hardship, occasionally making milk tea or using available ingredients to cook and improve their meals. Despite the tough conditions, the rich discoveries made during the surveys instantly alleviate our fatigue, replacing it with the excitement of finding artifacts. Occasionally discovering wild cactus fruits is also a rare pleasure during work.

After identifying Paleolithic sites, our members each became busy with their respective tasks: writing labels for lithics, taking photos of the site and surrounding landscape, recording the coordinates of the discovery locations, and so on. The team worked in a well-organized and orderly manner, with clear divisions of labor.

In 2017, during my work in Kenya, I was honored to meet the former President of Kenya, Mr. Moi. I still clearly remembered shaking hands with the President, who said slowly and deeply, "I like China very much, and I often go to Shanghai."

Throughout the four years of working in Kenya, every time we arrived or departed, the Chinese team members received invitations from our Embassy in Kenya. Walking through the embassy gate, I felt a profound sense of security, akin to returning home after a long period of traveling. Former Chinese Ambassadors to Kenya—Liu Xianfa, Zhang Gang, Liu Zhenyu, Cui Qing, and Li Meixuan—along with other diplomats, provided strong support for our work. Additionally, Mr. Han Ke and Mr. Kang Guodong from Chinese enterprises in the Baringo area offered significant assistance in our daily lives.

In 2019 and 2023, Zhang Huiming, Deputy Director of the Henan Provincial Administration of Cultural Heritage, and Wang Ruiqin, Division Chief of the Henan Provincial Administration of Cultural Heritage, led a delegation that traveled thousands of miles to visit the Lake Bogoria Site. They offered their greetings, provided guidance, and engaged in discussions with the leadership of the National Museums of Kenya. Our work garnered significant attention from Xinhua News Agency, China Central Television (CCTV), China Daily, and other media outlets in Kenya, resulting in extensive coverage. At the end of the 2023 field season, our archaeological team had the privilege of participating in a seminar at Xinhua News Agency's Africa Regional Bureau, thanks to an invitation from Mr. Ying Qiang, Mr. Li Wenfei, and Mr. Dai He of Xinhua News Agency.

The photos of the site were taken by Zhao Qingpo, Lou Wentai, Gu Xuejun and Job Kibii. All the stone artifacts shown in this book were photographed by Zhao Qingpo. The drawings of the stone artifacts were made by Zhao Qingpo and Peng Shenglan. Unwavering supports for the Sino-Kenya Paleolithic Archaeological Project were given by the leaders of National Cultural Heritage Administration of China, Henan Provincial Administration of Cultural Heritage, Henan Provincial Institute of Cultural Heritage and Archaeology, Luoyang City Cultural Relics and Archaeology Research Institute, the Embassy of the People's Republic of China in the Republic of Kenya and the National Museums of Kenya. The two project directors from Chinese side, Professor Li Zhanyang (2017 and 2018) and Senior Researcher Wei Xingtao (2019 and 2023), the two project leaders from Kenyan side, Job Kibii and Emmanuel Ndiema, as well as Director Liu Haiwang and Director Mary Gikungu all have strongly supported this project. I would like to express my sincere gratitude to all the leaders mentioned above and the workers who have participated in the Sino-Kenya Archaeological Project.

Zhao Qingpo

April 15, 2024

Henan Provincial Institute of Cultural Heritage and Archaeology
Academic Library Type B No.32

FROM HENAN TO EAST AFRICA SINO-KENYA PALEOLITHIC ARCHAEOLOGICAL PROJECT

A Study on Stone Artifacts from Lake Bogoria Site

ISBN 978-7-5010-8525-5

Price: 420.00RMB

Compiler

Henan Provincial Institute of Cultural Heritage and Archaeology

Luoyang City Cultural Relics and Archaeology Research Institute

National Museums of Kenya

Publishing Office

Cultural Relics Press

100007, Building 2, Beixiaojie, Dongzhimennei, Dongcheng District, Beijing, China

Tel: 86-10-64010048

Web: www.wenwu.com